GLOSSARY OF INSURANCE POLICY TERMS

ORGANISATION FOR ECONOMIC CO-OPERATION AND DEVELOPMENT

ORGANISATION FOR ECONOMIC CO-OPERATION AND DEVELOPMENT

Pursuant to Article 1 of the Convention signed in Paris on 14th December 1960, and which came into force on 30th September 1961, the Organisation for Economic Co-operation and Development (OECD) shall promote policies designed:

- to achieve the highest sustainable economic growth and employment and a rising standard of living in Member countries, while maintaining financial stability, and thus to contribute to the development of the world economy;
- to contribute to sound economic expansion in Member as well as non-member countries in the process of economic development; and
- to contribute to the expansion of world trade on a multilateral, non-discriminatory basis in accordance with international obligations.

The original Member countries of the OECD are Austria, Belgium, Canada, Denmark, France, Germany, Greece, Iceland, Ireland, Italy, Luxembourg, the Netherlands, Norway, Portugal, Spain, Sweden, Switzerland, Turkey, the United Kingdom and the United States. The following countries became Members subsequently through accession at the dates indicated hereafter: Japan (28th April 1964), Finland (28th January 1969), Australia (7th June 1971), New Zealand (29th May 1973), Mexico (18th May 1994), the Czech Republic (21st December 1995), Hungary (7th May 1996), Poland (22nd November 1996) and Korea (12th December 1996). The Commission of the European Communities takes part in the work of the OECD (Article 13 of the OECD Convention).

OECD CENTRE FOR CO-OPERATION WITH NON-MEMBERS

The OECD Centre for Co-operation with Non-Members (CCNM) was established in January 1998 when the OECD's Centre for Co-operation with the Economies in Transition (CCET) was merged with the Liaison and Co-ordination Unit (LCU). The CCNM, in combining the functions of these two entities, serves as the focal point for the development and pursuit of co-operation between the OECD and non-member economies.

The CCNM manages thematic and country programmes. The thematic programmes, which are multi-country in focus, are linked to the core generic work areas of the Organisation (such as trade and investment, taxation, labour market and social policies, environment). The Emerging Market Economy Forum (EMEF) and the Transition Economy Programme (TEP) provide the framework for activities under the thematic programmes. The EMEF is a flexible forum in which non-members are invited to participate depending on the theme under discussion. The TEP is focused exclusively on transition economies. Regional/Country programmes, providing more focused dialogue and assistance, are now in place for the Baltic countries, Brazil, Bulgaria, China, Romania, Russia, the Slovak Republic (a candidate for accession to the OECD), and Slovenia.

FOREWORD

This glossary aims at providing simple and easily comprehensible explanations of the main regulatory and supervisory insurance terms used in most OECD countries. Readers will also find helpful illustrations of important, related policy and technical issues.

The publication is intended as a practical tool for government insurance officials, academic and business communities as well as journalists worldwide. It is hoped that it will contribute to mutual understanding and policy dialogue, two key objectives of OECD's co-operation with non-Member economies. It is one of the many significant initiatives undertaken by the OECD Insurance Committee, under the aegis of the Centre for Co-operation with Non-Member countries (CCNM).

Readers will find specific references to individual OECD countries and cross references to the OECD Insurance Guidelines for Economies in Transition and related OECD publications (see the annex and bibliography). The glossary complements the publication *Insurance Regulation and Supervision in OECD Countries* (1999) which contains an extensive analysis of regulatory and supervisory systems in OECD countries.

The OECD Insurance and Private Pensions Unit prepared this glossary, based on contributions from Professor Harold D. Skipper, Jr. (Georgia State University) and Professor Guy Simonet (Institut libre des finances et des assurances). Mr. Hidekatsu Sekiguchi (Insurance and Private Pensions Unit) edited and compiled the glossary with the editorial assistance of Mr. Edward Smiley. It also benefited from the expertise of the Task Force of the Insurance Committee on Insurance Regulation. The OECD Internet Site, *www.oecd.org* contains more information on OECD insurance activities.

The views expressed here do not necessarily reflect those of the Insurance Committee or the Member countries. It is published on the responsibility of the Secretary-General of the OECD.

Eric Burgeat
Director
Centre for Co-operation with Non-Members

The Table of Contents lists the main insurance terms defined by this glossary and which are shown in **boldfaced type**. Additional terms are defined within the discussions of the main terms and appear in ***boldfaced, italicised type***. Terms are given their most common definition, with variations provided. Where more than a single term may be frequently used for the definition, the other terms are noted. All terms are indexed at the end of the glossary, enabling readers to locate a specific term or expression. The boldfaced page numbers shown in the index refer the reader to the main definition of the term.

TABLE OF CONTENTS

ACCOUNTING PRINCIPLES

[*See also "OECD Insurance Guidelines" in the Annex, and "Insurance Regulation and Supervision in Economies in Transition (1997)".*]

Accounting principles are the standards required or expected to be followed by insurers in preparing their financial statements. Standards may be promulgated by the national accounting association (or organisation sponsored by or associated with the association), by a government agency or by both. Standards established by a national association are sometimes referred to as ***generally accepted accounting principles (GAAP)***. Standards set by the insurance regulatory authority or the insurance law are sometimes referred to as ***statutory*** (or ***regulatory) accounting principles (SAP*** or ***RAP)***. The national tax authority may require use of its own accounting principles, and the insurer itself may follow other accounting principles designed for optimum management.

Insurance accounting principles establish asset and liability valuation standards. Usually, assets are carried on insurer balance sheets either at 1) the lower of their market value or their original cost or 2) their market value. The methods and assumptions used to derive **life insurance provisions** may be prescribed in great detail or the regulator may rely on the company's or on an independent actuarial valuation. The requirements typically result in a conservative assessment (*i.e.*, overstatement) of insurers' liabilities.

National laws are more general for non-life insurers' reserves (provisions). **Provisions for unearned premiums** (or unearned premium reserves) may be prescribed in some detail and calculated as a prorated share on a gross premium basis or on **premiums** net of acquisition **expenses**. Appropriate establishment of **provisions for outstanding claims** (or loss reserves) has been a regulatory challenge. Detailed reporting schedules may be required or reporting may be more general. The discounting of loss reserves is not, in general, practised. Some countries make no *provisions for claims incurred but not reported (IBNR).* The EU Insurance Accounts Directive (both life and non-life) establishes minimum standards for the presentation and valuation of assets and liabilities. Its intent is to render national insurance accounting within the EU more comparable. The directive requires that accounts give a "true and fair view" of the company's financial activities. It allows assets to be carried either at their market value or at historical cost. If the historical cost approach is adopted, market values must be shown in notes, and vice versa. The EU directive largely permits countries to continue or establish their own reserving practices. [See **TECHNICAL PROVISIONS (RESERVES)**]

Accounting standards extend also to insurers' income statements (profit and loss accounts). Differences arise in whether a distinction is made between underwriting (technical) results and investment (non-technical) results and the mechanism for recognising realised and unrealised capital gains and losses. The EU accounts directive requires realised gains and losses to be brought into the operating statement and it allows countries to decide whether to permit or require acquisition expenses to be written off immediately or deferred. Apart from the EU, a variety of accounting practices exist internationally regarding the treatment of policy acquisition costs, with some countries requiring their immediate write off and others requiring varying degrees of capitalisation and amortisation.

In addition, some countries permit insurers and reinsurers great latitude in how they use their reserves relative to the income statement. Cross-country comparisons of insurer income statements, therefore, can be complex.

One principle upon which most observers agree is, however, that financial statements should be optimally useful for their intended audiences. Thus, individuals interested in purchasing shares of an insurer would be interested in the firm's value as an operating entity, including embedded values within the insurer's various books of business. Insurance regulators, on the other hand, would be more interested in the insurer's **liquidation** value

There is still a large variety of accounting principles in OECD countries. Although accounting has to take into account national characteristics, this heterogeneity has adverse effects on current trends toward further internationalisation and globalisation and create major obstacles for adequate supervision of insurers. Recent works have been undertaken toward the promotion of common standards, in particular by the IASC (International Accounting Standards Committee).

AUTHORISATION

[*See also "OECD Insurance Guidelines" in the Annex, "Insurance Regulation and Supervision in Economies in Transition (1997), "Insurance Solvency Supervision (1995)", and "Policy Issues in Insurance (1993)"*.]

An insurer is said to be ***authorised*** or ***admitted*** if it has received the permission of the insurance supervisory authority to conduct business within the supervisor's jurisdiction. Ordinarily, **authorisation** occurs through registration or licensing. The purpose of requiring authorisation is to protect the public. Most countries limit the purchase of the compulsory classes of insurance (*e.g.*, motor third party liability) to authorised insurers. Most countries prohibit insurers from engaging in the business of insurance within their jurisdiction without authorisation. Many countries also prohibit their citizens and businesses from purchasing non-compulsory classes of insurance from unauthorised insurers. Some countries allow their citizens and businesses to purchase non-compulsory classes of insurance from any insurer. (see **COMPULSORY INSURANCE**)

The issues associated with authorisation are similar to those of **cross-border insurance trade**; *i.e.*, to protect uninformed insurance purchasers. Another issue relates to the government's ability to tax. Taxing unauthorised insurers can be difficult or even impossible. Some countries tax them indirectly through the intermediaries which represent them. (see **TAXATION OF INSURANCE PRODUCTS**)

In the EU, insurance and similar activities are subject to prior "administrative authorisation," based on technical considerations (see **BUSINESS PLAN**), granted by the supervisory authorities of the Member State of origin when an insurance company is set up in that State, or when an existing company wishes to extend the types of insurance it offers in a given class or to do business in new classes.

Companies whose head office is located in a State that is not a Member of the European Economic Area must also request a "special authorisation," based on policy considerations, for the general agents representing them.

The administrative authorisation granted by one Member State is valid throughout the entire EU and allows companies either to establish themselves in other EU States or to provide insurance services directly from the

State of origin. Authorisation must be obtained for each class of insurance, whether for a class as a whole or for certain risks contained within it. Authorisation may also be granted for a group of risks involving more than one class. For example, authorisation for motor vehicle insurance includes the "injury to passengers" risk within the "accident" class. In turn, this class includes "land motor vehicles," "goods in transit," and "land motor vehicle liability." Ancillary risks from another class or group of classes also may be covered without specific authorisation if they are related to the main risk, concern the subject matter of the main risk, and are included in the contract covering the main risk.

BROKERS

[*See also "OECD Insurance Guidelines" in the Annex.*]

As mentioned in the definition of **distribution systems**, **brokers** represent the insurance purchaser, are expected to be knowledgeable about the overall insurance market, and tend to work with large clients. An insurance broker solicits business from the public under no employment from any particular **insurance company**, and places insurance with insurers chosen by the insured with the advice of the broker.

Insurance brokers play an important role in commercial insurance in most OECD countries. Business firms often have unique property or liability exposures, or require insurance contracts written to their own specifications. Brokers often help write insurance specifications or even design the insurance program and then find an insurer willing to provide the coverage. In many cases, brokers supply additional services such as providing **risk management** and loss control advice and helping their clients file claims after losses. Business firms often employ brokers when insuring their employee benefit plans, such as their group life and health insurance.

In **reinsurance**, brokers also play an important role as intermediaries. The reinsurance broker is to 1) place at the disposal of the direct-writing company an array of reinsurance companies, 2) provide wider market knowledge, and 3) impart impartial, experienced counsel.

The changes in the business environment have resulted in changes in brokers' traditional roles. The changes in the relationships between their clients and the insurance companies with which they place business have affected broker revenues. In addition, pressure from external competitors threatens their traditional role.

Traditionally, brokers have earned the great majority of their revenues through commissions paid to them by the insurers with whom they place business. Commissions remain an important revenue source, especially for small to medium sized brokers. However, the large national and international brokerage firms within the OECD countries are today emphasising their advisory roles in addition to their purely insurance placement role, and, in the process, are placing greater reliance on fee-based income. They have established significant risk management consultancy operations to provide advice to customers on everything from loss control to captive insurer formation and management.

Large brokerage customers today are unwilling to support payment to the broker of commissions at the rates that were paid in the past. They are demanding demonstrations of the "value added" by the broker to the insurance transaction in return for commissions. Also, with an increasing reliance on various self-retention methods large firms have less need for traditional brokerage services. Many customers no longer will agree to a commission arrangement, instead paying brokers for their advice and counsel directly or even creating performance-based compensation arrangements.

A consequence of these trends has been great pressure on broker revenues and a corresponding movement to lower operating **expenses**. In turn, this has led and is expected to continue to lead to substantial world-wide consolidation among brokers.

BUSINESS PLAN

[*See also "OECD Insurance Guidelines" in the Annex*.]

The **business plan** allows both the company to demonstrate its ability to make appropriate estimations for future three-to-five years activities and the supervisor to assess the relevance of such estimations. The business plan is a key element of licensing process.

In the EU, for instance, the business plan is one of the documents that must accompany all **authorisation** applications. It comprises the following items:

1. a description of the kinds of risks that the company proposes to cover, or the commitments that it intends to undertake;

2. a **reinsurance** plan setting down the company's intended guidelines with regard to reinsurance, and a list of the main reinsurers it has contacted, accompanied by documentary evidence of its intention to sign contracts with those companies;

3. justification of the components of the minimum guaranty fund;

4. an estimate of the cost of setting up administrative services and a production network, together with an estimate of the financial resources available to meet this cost; in addition, companies intending to engage in assistance insurance activities must show that they have the necessary staff and equipment to meet their commitments.

Companies are also asked to provide estimates for the first three financial years in respect of:

- administrative **expenses** other than set-up costs, especially ordinary overheads and commissions;

- **premiums** and claims for direct business, gross risks accepted and risks ceded to reinsurers;

- the financial resources available to cover commitments and the solvency margin;

- the cash flow situation.

It should be mentioned that some countries require estimates for five financial years.

The following additional information is required of non-EU companies:

- the general and special terms of the policies proposed;

- the premiums that the company intends to charge, or the technical basis on which it will determine its premiums, for each category of transaction, for both life and non-life companies (this additional information is not required for damage cover in the transport class, except for land vehicles, nor for goods in transport, and it may not be required for aircraft liability; the amount of premiums is not required for credit and suretyship risks. For life activities, the technical basis must contain the necessary elements for calculating premiums and **technical provisions**).

– the balance sheets and profit and loss accounts of the last three years, if available, or, if not, of the most recent complete financial years.

The company must submit a regular report to the competent supervisory authorities showing that it is complying with its business plan.

CLAIMS INCURRED

[*See also "OECD Insurance Guidelines" in the Annex and "Insurance Regulation and Supervision in Economies in Transition (1997)".*]

This component of the profit and loss account is equal to the algebraic sum of the following items:

1. payments to policyholders and beneficiaries of various benefits, *e.g.* indemnities, capital, annuities, surrenders, etc., less recoveries from third parties (subrogation) and salvage;

2. changes in the **provision for outstanding claims** and in the estimation of recoveries between the end of the previous financial year and the end of the current year;

3. **expenses** attributable to claims, such as fees paid to doctors, experts, officers of the court, etc. Depending on the legislation, these expenses may include internal costs only (*e.g.* salaries of claims adjusters and inspectors) or both internal and external costs (*e.g.* external adjusters, etc.).

From a technical standpoint, **claims incurred** can be assessed by occurrence or by underwriting year, and from an accounting standpoint, by financial year. In particular, insurers monitor and analyse changes in claims incurred in an underwriting year (n) as they age in years (n), (n+1), (n+2), etc., whereas in accounting terms they consider the total incurred losses of the financial year (in which claims were recorded).

The ***claims ratio***, computed by dividing claims incurred by earned premiums, is one of the most important indicators of non-life insurers' underwriting performance.

COMPETITION (ANTITRUST) REGULATION

[***See also "OECD Insurance Guidelines" in the Annex.***]

Competition (antitrust) regulation is a nation's laws and regulations that govern private producers' behaviour and the market structure within which interactions between producers take place. Competition regulation addresses anti-competitive practices of individual firms (*e.g.*, pricing matters) as well as competition-reducing arrangements between firms.

Insurers can use several methods to lessen competition. They can collude in setting rates, in using particular policy forms, or in a host of other activities. Through mergers or acquisitions, insurers can gain market power, thus restraining competition. Finally, insurers already in dominant positions within their marketplaces can abuse this power through tie-in arrangements, by withholding capacity, or by a range of other competition-reducing activities. National insurance laws and **regulations** typically seek to punish or prohibit anti-competitive behaviour by establishing 1) rules against collusive practices, 2) rules against mergers or acquisitions that restrict competition, and 3) rules against abuse of dominant position.

A distinguishing characteristic of competition laws internationally is their broad formulation and brevity. As a result, regulators and the courts enjoy a wide margin of discretion in their application. Countries usually take a pragmatic position on enforcement. Thus, the usual position is that anti-competitive behaviour is permitted provided the positive economic effects seem to dominate the negative. Hence, bureau data gathering and distribution and form promulgation may be permitted although such actions are co-operative.

Competition laws and provisions are structured around the principle of prohibition or the principle of abuse, with most countries relying on both. Under the ***principle of prohibition***, enumerated behaviour such as hard core cartels and resale price maintenance is deemed anti-competitive and automatically illegal. It is illegal *per se*. Under the ***principle of abuse***, an inquiry into the economic effects of the alleged offensive behaviour, other than those mentioned above, is required. Only with a finding of damaging effects can the activity be declared illegal.

Within the EU, mergers and other concentration activities must be pre-notified to the European Commission. The Commission has issued certain "block exemptions" with respect to certain otherwise offensive behaviour. These cover:

- The development of common pure (*i.e.*, no loadings) risk **premiums**
- The elaboration of common standard policy provisions
- Common coverage (*e.g.*, coinsurance or co-reinsurance pools) for certain exposures
- Common rules for testing and acceptance of security devices

Competition law can be expected to gain in importance as markets liberalise and deregulate. Because of differences in laws and enforcement, national competition policy itself is becoming an important trade issue.

COMPULSORY INSURANCE

[*See also "OECD Insurance Guidelines" in the Annex and "Insurance Regulation and Supervision in Economies in Transition (1997)".*]

Compulsory insurance is any form of insurance whose purchase is required by law. Governments typically require the purchase of liability insurance with respect to three types of potential loss-causing activities: 1) those whose severity could be particularly great, with the possibility of large numbers of innocent persons being harmed because of a single event, 2) those whose frequency is sufficiently great to affect large numbers of innocent persons independently, and 3) those that are judged to be inherently dangerous.

Activities within the first category which commonly require the purchase of liability insurance include operation of nuclear powered electrical generation facilities, petroleum shipments via land and sea, and aircraft operation. Although the frequency of these types of losses is relatively low, they have the potential for causing catastrophic harm when they do occur. Because of the high losses that could be imposed on third parties, governments have determined that those engaged in such activities should be held responsible for resulting losses. Also, they should be able to demonstrate financial responsibility prior to any loss, typically in the form of a liability insurance policy with certain minimum limits. Otherwise, it might be too easy for firms engaging in these activities to escape liability by declaring bankruptcy or otherwise insulating themselves against liability.

In the second category, we find that liability cover is required in all or almost all OECD countries in connection with motor vehicle operation. Here the concern is not that a single loss-causing event will cause great damage, as with events in the first category, but that such relatively high frequency events collectively could impose significant costs on third parties. Without compulsory motor vehicle liability insurance, it could be too easy for large numbers of motor vehicle operators to escape liability by declaring bankruptcy or being judgement proof (*i.e.* being unable to pay any judgement). Due to increasing numbers of automobiles and drivers, the number of accidents is expected to grow, and resulting carnage could have severe economic and social effects on accident victims and their families. [see **POLICYHOLDER PROTECTION FUND (INSURANCE GUARANTY FUND)**]

Finally, governments routinely require the purchase of liability insurance or the showing of other financial responsibility in connection with activities that are deemed to be inherently dangerous. Activities falling within this category include the use and transport of hazardous substances, such as explosives, and hunting.

Not included in the definition of compulsory insurance are the many social insurance programs sponsored by governments, participation in which is compulsory. With social insurance programs, the concern is with income redistribution and with protecting people against their own failure, for whatever reason, to prepare adequately for adverse personal events.

CONTRACT LAW

[*See also "OECD Insurance Guidelines" in the Annex and "Policy Issues in Insurance (1993)".*]

Insurance contracts are traditionally divided into two categories of insurance, *i.e.* **non-life** and **life insurance**.

The former pays for the cost of repairing or replacing property, while the second grants a predetermined benefit in the event of death (or survival, in "supplementary insurance" added to a life assurance policy).

The term of a non-life insurance policy is generally one year, with the option of (automatic) renewal by ***tacit agreement***, or it may have a medium-term duration (*e.g.* three years in France and Sweden); in life and health insurance, however, long-term policies are dominant.

Under the ***principle of indemnity***, the amount paid by an insurer cannot exceed the loss sustained, to avoid having the insured make a profit on the event in question. Nevertheless, so-called ***new for old*** provisions make it possible to pay claims without deduction for wear and tear. Another provision is related to cumulative, multiple or double insurance, making a distinction between good faith and bad faith ; it also refers to malicious damage .

Once a loss is paid to the insured, there is a legal transfer to the insurer of the insured's right to take action against responsible parties, up to the amount paid under the relevant policy: this mechanism is called ***subrogation***. In respect of personal insurance, however, these principles do not apply, except in the case of malicious damage.

Most often, insurance cover is provisionally given by the company in exchange for remittance of a ***proposal form***, which becomes definitive when the applicant returns a signed policy to the company. But in Italy, for example, cover will be maintained, for a certain period, until the policy is signed. In some countries, the ***effective date*** (on which cover becomes effective) may be different from the date of the contract.

Payment of the first **premium** generally triggers cover by the insurer, *e.g.* as stipulated in EC directives. In Italy, however, if an insurer does not require this payment, neither does it guarantee the contract. In Switzerland, if a company issues a policy before the first premium is paid, it means that the cover is effective regardless of whether the insured pays the premium thereafter.

Another issue is the place where the premium should be paid:

- at the office of insurer or its intermediary; or,
- at the address of the policyholder.

Moreover, the intervention of an intermediary could give rise to a dispute over payment of the premium unless it is agreed in advance.

The principle is to refuse cover when premiums are not paid on time, but legislation in several countries provides that this sanction is applied only after an insurer has issued a warning and served advance notice. As a rule, days of grace are granted either by law or under the contract; thereafter, the contract is cancelled.

A ***risk-assessment questionnaire*** may also be included in the proposal form. In Latin countries, such a document supplies full details needed to evaluate the risk covered. If the insured amount is lower than the actual value of the property as determined from the questionnaire, the amount of the claim payout will be reduced in proportion to the under-evaluation by application of an ***average condition*** coefficient.

Should a risk increase, the policyholder is generally required to so inform the insurer. The policyholder may then cancel the contract due to the resultant rise in the premium. If a risk decreases, some countries allow a reduction in the premium or, if necessary, cancellation of the policy.

The following risks are typically excluded:

- arson and other intentional acts which are wrongful and unlawful;
- gross negligence though without wrongful intention;
- catastrophic events: some countries have legislation with specific provisions excluding catastrophic events and the consequences of war, riots and civil disturbances.

In the event of a loss, the policyholder shall inform the insurer of the event, "immediately", "as soon as possible" or "within a fixed period", after the event has become known to him.

Some policies may include a condition which, in the event of a claim, requires the policyholder to bear a portion of the claim "for his own account", either as a flat amount or a given percentage. This sharing of a loss is called ***franchise*** when it applies to a loss that is less than or equal to the specified amount, and ***deductible*** when the specified amount is always deducted, regardless of the amount of the loss.

CROSS-BORDER INSURANCE TRADE

[*See also "OECD Insurance Guidelines" in the Annex and "Liberalisation of International Insurance Operations (1999)".*]

Cross-border insurance trade exists when a non-resident insurance provider sells insurance to residents. From the point of view of the insurer's country of domicile (its ***home country***), such insurance is an export. From the point of view of the country of residence of the insured person or object (the ***host country***), the insurance is an import. Cross-border insurance trade can take several forms, the more important of which are discussed below.

Pure cross-border insurance trade exists when the resultant insurance contract is entered into because of solicitations by a foreign insurer. The solicitation may have been via direct response techniques (*e.g.*, telephone, newspaper, mail, Internet, etc.) or **brokers**. Such insurance typically involves large risks. Much **reinsurance** is marketed in this way.

Own-initiative cross-border insurance trade means that the insured initiated the contact with the insurer. Corporations often seek insurance abroad trying to secure more favourable terms, conditions or prices than those available locally. Individuals less frequently will do so. A distinction should be made between such own-initiative insurance wherein the insured has no relationship with the insurer and where the foreign insurer is owned by the insured (*i.e.*, captive insurer).

Consumption-abroad cross-border insurance trade occurs when an insured, temporarily resident or visiting abroad, enters into an insurance contract with a local insurer. A distinction should be noted between such purchases intended to provide cover only during the length of stay and insurance intended for long term coverage.

Yet another variation of cross-border insurance trade is seen when a multinational corporation (MNC) purchases ***difference-in-conditions (DIC)***

insurance or ***difference-in-limits (DIL) insurance*** as part of its global risk management program. These "global" policies enable levelling of different policy conditions or insurance limits provided by local policies. Such policies, usually written in the MNC's home country, may involve coinsurance with foreign or other domestic insurers.

Economists would argue that, in an ideal world, complete freedom would be extended to insurers (and reinsurers) to provide cross-border insurance services and to customers to purchase insurance from whomever they wished. In practice, however, two sets of problems are said to argue against the position.

First, many, especially developing, countries have argued that cross-border insurance trade has negative macroeconomic effects on the national economy. In contrast to insurance purchased from locally established insurers which then invest funds locally to back their reserve obligations -- thus aiding economic development -- cross-border insurance purchases usually result in little or no domestic investment. In addition, cross-border trade can result in less local insurance expertise creation (technology transfer) than **establishment insurance trade**.

The issue, however, is more complex than the above simple analysis suggests, as important secondary effects should be considered. If the national market fails to offer desired coverage because of insufficient local capacity or because of pricing or product availability problems, forcing customers to purchase inferior coverage locally may be self-defeating longer term. Thus, the argument against cross-border insurance trade based on pleas for enhanced local investment and technology transfer does not enjoy unambiguous support.

The *second* argument against complete freedom for cross-border insurance trade focuses on consumer protection. Because of the close tie that insurance has with the overall public interest and its quasi-fiduciary nature, governments world-wide have been reluctant to ignore the natural imbalance in positions between certain insurance buyers and sellers. Sophisticated insurance buyers, such as large businesses, have reasonable opportunity to become well-informed buyers and to avoid financially weak or incompetent insurers. The need for government oversight is correspondingly less. The same logic applies when direct insurers purchase reinsurance.

The situation with individual consumers and small businesses is different. They are more likely to be misled or to fail to know enough even to make appropriate inquiries as they negotiate for insurance. It is for this reason that governments world-wide insist on licensing and seek particularly to protect the least informed among insurance buyers. These same concerns do not apply with well-informed buyers.

An exception to this view can occur when the insurance regulator of the customer's state is satisfied that the insurer's home country regulation provides protection to the customer, which is at least equivalent to that which the customer's state provides. This ***mutual recognition*** approach underpins the EU's Single Market Program.

DEMUTUALISATION

Demutualisation is the process by which a mutual **insurance company** is converted into a stock insurance company. The distinguishing characteristic of a ***mutual insurance company*** is that it is owned by and operated for the exclusive benefit of its policyholders. Corporate ownership is imputed through policy ownership. A ***stock insurance company***, by contrast, is owned by its shareholders who need not be policyholders.

With an increasing emphasis on financial solidity in many markets, insurers have placed greater stress on their capital positions. Additionally, many observers believe that successful financial intermediaries in the future must be larger, must be capable of creating or acquiring other firms and must expand into new areas -- each of which requires more capital. Most often, the only means by which mutual insurance companies can raise additional capital is through retained earnings. By contrast, stock insurance companies can raise new capital by retaining earnings and issuing new shares. This fact gives the stock corporate form advantages over the mutual form.

Mutual insurers, therefore, may have incentives to convert to stock insurers to be able to raise additional capital in order to be able to compete more effectively. Also, demutualisation could allow for enhanced corporate flexibility through use of upstream holding companies. Through this mechanism, the company can limit the impact of insurance regulatory controls and restrictions on non-insurance operations, and permit fewer constraints on insurance company acquisitions.

The demutualisation process often involves three phases.

First, the mutual insurer's board of directors determines that demutualisation is in the policyholders' best interests.

1. Second, governmental approval is required. This decision to approve will be assessed on whether the proposal provides adequately for existing and future policyholders, the fairness of the consideration to policyholders in exchange for their membership rights, the allocation of the consideration among policyholders, the fairness of the amounts paid by non-policyholder shareholders (particularly in the case of a proposed acquisition of the company by another entity), and the limitations on acquisitions of stock by officers and directors. Public hearings may be required.

2. Once the company and the government official have agreed on a conversion plan, they submit it to policyholders for approval. If a favourable vote is received, the process may continue.

An important issue in a demutualisation is how it will affect insurance coverage of persons with participating policies. Some have argued that a conversion should not have a materially adverse impact on the company's ability either to meet the policy guarantees or to pay policyholder dividends on a scale comparable to those that they would have paid lacking demutualisation.

A recent move in the United States has been for the states to allow mutuals to secure capital through creation of a new holding company structure. This structure permits the raising of equity capital.

DISTRIBUTION SYSTEMS

[*See also "OECD Insurance Guidelines" in the Annex*.]

In insurance, **distribution systems** are the means by which insurance policies are sold to customers. Insurance is sold in one or a combination of three ways: direct response, agents or **brokers**. Thus, some insurers sell directly to customers (***direct response***) via the Internet, mail, telephone solicitation, newspaper advertisements or other direct means, without the use of intermediaries. Relatively little insurance is sold world-wide through such direct solicitation, although the proportion is growing in some European markets, especially in motor insurance.

Perhaps the majority of both **life** and **non-life insurance** world-wide is sold through agents and brokers. Brokers represent the insurance purchaser. Brokers are expected to be knowledgeable about the overall insurance market and tend to work with large clients.

Two broad classes of agents are found internationally. Agents who sell exclusively for one insurer are referred to as ***captive, exclusive*** or ***tied agents***. ***Independent agents*** represent several insurers. Insurance brokers, and also independent agents, reinforce product and price competition by rectifying, to some extent, the information imbalance between the buyer and seller.

Banks, which can use any of the above distribution systems, are important insurance outlets in some markets. In the majority of instances, the bank serves as an agent for either an affiliated insurer or an insurer with whom the bank has a special arrangement. The latter situation is less common. In no OECD country are banks broadly permitted to underwrite insurance directly, although most countries permit them to do so through holding company arrangements. (see **FINANCIAL SERVICES CONGLOMERATES**)

Insurance distribution channels are vitally important to new entrants -- both foreign and domestic. The lack of reasonably developed brokerage or independent agency distribution systems in markets can constitute a structural entry barrier.

Consumer protection concerns flow from insurer marketing efforts. Where distribution is via local establishment, such as an agency, branch or subsidiary, local regulation and a **national treatment** standard might be sufficient. Cross-border distribution, on the other hand, may not ensure local consumers adequate protection against marketing abuses. The issue of adequate consumer protection from marketing abuses may warrant little government concern in respect to **reinsurance** or commercial insurance lines. Individuals are arguably more vulnerable to such abuses, and a mechanism to ensure host-country protection may be warranted in a liberalised insurance world. In many markets, insurance salespeople must register or secure a license. To obtain a license, the individual may be required to pass a qualifying examination, exhibit certain experience and be sponsored by an insurer. (see **CROSS-BORDER INSURANCE TRADE**)

EARNED PREMIUMS

[*See also "OECD Insurance Guidelines" in the Annex and "Insurance Regulation and Supervision in Economies in Transition (1997)".*]

The principle of independent accounting periods, under which revenue and expenses should be charged exclusively to the period in which they are incurred, is applied only to insurance business, in particular through the concept of **earned premiums** and the corresponding **expenses**, which are known as **claims incurred**.

From an accounting standpoint, calculating earned premiums for a given year involves determining the total amount of premiums covering risks for the period from 1 January through 31 December, *i.e.* the algebraic sum of the following three elements:

1. the portion of **premiums** written in prior accounting periods and providing coverage in the current year [*i.e.* ***premiums brought forward*** from previous year(s)];

2. premiums written during the current year at the beginning of the period of coverage (*i.e.* current-year premiums written in advance); *less*

3. the portion of premiums written in the current and/or prior years and providing coverage in the following and/or subsequent years (*i.e.* ***premiums to be carried forward*** to the following year or to subsequent years).

These elements, which are net of cancelled premiums, should exclude any taxes on premiums.

In addition, estimates of the following have to be booked as valuation adjustments:

1. premiums yet to be written, *inter alia*, for contracts with notice at the end of the period of coverage;

2. current-year premiums yet to be cancelled on account of errors or irrecoverability.

In the event that rates should prove insufficient because of aggravated loss experience and/or increased administrative expenses, earned premiums must be reduced by the amount needed to cover the supplementary risks and administrative costs. This is done by virtue of the **accounting principle** of prudence, so that potential losses incurred during the current year are not transferred to the next. In EU terminology, this supplement is referred to as the **provision for unexpired risks**.

The concept of earned premiums can be approached in two different ways:

1. from a purely technical standpoint, based on the current underwriting year, *i.e.* disregarding premiums written or cancelled in respect of previous years. Here, changes in earned premiums for an underwriting year (n) may be observed in various accounting years [(n), (n+1), (n+2), etc.], since items estimated the first year -- premiums yet to be written or cancelled -- will be booked in subsequent accounting periods as different amounts.

2. from a purely accounting standpoint, based on the current accounting period, *i.e.* on the profit and loss account (as defined in the EU layout).

In either case, earned premiums may be taken gross or net of **reinsurance** and computed in reference to either gross premiums or risk premiums, *i.e.* with acquisition costs deducted. It should be noted that a similar concept can be used in **life insurance** by adjusting premiums written for the change in unearned premiums included in the **life insurance provision**.

EQUALISATION PROVISION OR RESERVE

[***See also "Insurance Solvency Supervision (1995)".***]

This valuation adjustment smoothes out non-life profits.

- for certain seasonal or cyclical risks, such as hail, natural disasters, space or nuclear risks, pollution liability or credit insurance; or,
- for an insurer's entire portfolio.

A number of countries substitute mandatory **reinsurance** for this technical requirement. The names by which it is known are many and varied: **equalisation provision or reserve**, **provision for differential loss experience**, **for disasters**, but also **contingency**, **safety** or **fluctuation reserve**, **equalisation fund**, etc. Whether it is treated as a provision or a reserve, the fund is not considered part of the solvency margin.

Insurers believe that the use of such funds is fully justified because of the volatile nature of some of their risks: the results of a single year will not necessarily be representative of other years, especially if catastrophic claims distort those results. The fund is tacit recognition that the diversification of some insured risks is impaired by the independent nature thereof, and a long-term view of the insurance business justifies such reserves.

On the other hand, some public policymakers argue that this volatility is an inherent risk of the insurance business and should be priced accordingly. The issue relates less to whether insurers should voluntarily establish such reserves or be compelled to do so than to whether insurers that do establish such reserves should be entitled to a tax deduction because of them. Here the argument is that, since the insurer has not actually incurred the loss at the time it creates or adds to the reserve, it should not be able to deduct such reserves until such time as losses are actually paid.

In the EU, the provision can function in one of two ways:

1. as an accounting mechanism: A given percentage of technical profit is set aside to constitute a fund, up to a certain ceiling expressed in terms of **premiums** written. Both the percentage and the ceiling vary by class, according to the nature of the risk involved. Calculations are carried out net of reinsurance. Any technical losses are charged in full to the fund, the value of which cannot, however, be less than zero.

2. as an actuarial mechanism: Additions to the provision are calculated with reference to **earned premiums** and defined by the positive variance on loss experience, *i.e.* the amount by which the average loss experience over a reference period spanning the past 15 or 30 years exceeds actual loss experience. If actual losses are above average, the difference is charged to the fund. In addition, and independently of these movements, the fund is credited with interest payments which are computed by applying a fixed rate of

interest to the fund's theoretical ceiling. The ceiling is determined by multiplying earned premiums by {n} times the standard deviation of loss experience over the reference period. The fund may be subject to a minimum value, which would also be computed using the standard deviation.

ESTABLISHMENT INSURANCE TRADE

[*See also "Liberalisation of International Insurance Operations (1999)".*]

Establishment insurance trade exists when insurance is sold to residents through local agencies, branches or subsidiaries owned by non-residents. The opportunity to establish a local presence is often essential to the efficient provision of insurance services. The conditions of establishment determine whether non-resident enterprises can compete with each other and with domestic firms on an equal footing. Establishment insurance trade can take several forms, the most important of which are discussed below.

Establishment via ***subsidiary*** exists when non-residents create a *de novo* domestic insurer or acquire an existing domestic insurer. Excepting ownership nationality differences, such subsidiaries are legally identical to other national insurers and, therefore, answer fully to the national insurance regulator -- not the owner's domiciliary regulator.

The next most substantive form of establishment is through creation of a ***branch office***. A branch office is a detached portion of a foreign insurer. Unlike a subsidiary, the branch office is not a standalone insurer, but legally a part of an insurer. As such, the branch office is subject to home country regulatory oversight. Because it incurs financial obligations locally and itself typically bears risk locally, it is also subject to host-country **regulation**. This dual regulatory oversight can lead to conflicts of law and regulation.

Insurers sometimes seek foreign establishment through creation of an ***agency***. An agency is the least substantial form of risk-bearing establishment. As the legal representative of the foreign insurer, the agent's powers to represent its principal may be narrow (*e.g.*, sales only) or broad (*e.g.*, sales, underwriting, pricing and claim settlement). The foreign-owned domestic agency must comply fully with all host country agent licensing and other requirements. Establishment by agency is akin to **cross-border insurance**

trade as the actual risk is borne by a foreign insurer not subject to host-country control.

As a fourth form of establishment, a ***representative office*** seeks to promote the interests of and sometimes services the local clients of the foreign insurer. The representative office neither bears risk nor sells insurance. Usually, its establishment does not require host country regulatory approval although notification is required.

Establishment has long been among the most contentious insurance trade issues, although OECD code obligations, the newly adopted GATS and a general world-wide liberalisation trend have all softened the intensity of the debate recently. One of the reasons for this intensity is that establishment requires (in the more substantive cases) foreign direct investment (FDI), and FDI historically has been closely associated with the exercise of national sovereignty.

Establishment issues stem principally from **market access**, **national treatment** and **transparency** concerns. Thus, some countries have limited foreign insurer market access via establishment because of a desire to protect the local insurance industry and because of concerns about excessive competition. Even when market access is not a problem, foreign-owned establishments may be denied national treatment, thus placing them at a competitive disadvantage. Finally, in some markets, transparency problems exist in that market access and other competitive rules may be unwritten, incomplete or inconsistently enforced.

EXPENSES

For an **insurance company**, the ***profit and loss account*** is composed of:

1. a technical component: **premium** income as profit, and **claims incurred** (including loss adjustment expenses) as loss;

2. a financial component: symmetrically, investment income and investment expenses;

3. other components:

- recurrent expenses, such as acquisition costs and administrative costs;
- non-recurrent expenses and income, which are often called ***exceptional items***.

What is generally termed **expenses** is the total of the following four recurrent items:

1. ***Acquisition costs***: the costs arising from the conclusion of insurance contracts and comprising:
   - direct costs, such as *a)* acquisition and renewal commissions (renewal commissions may be included in administrative expenses) and *b)* the cost of drawing up insurance documents or including insurance contracts in a portfolio.
   - indirect costs, such as advertising costs or the administrative expenses connected with the processing of proposals and the issuing of policies.

2. ***Administrative expenses***: Administrative expenses consist essentially of costs arising from: *a)* premium collection; *b)* portfolio administration; *c)* handling of bonuses and rebates; *d)* inward and outward **reinsurance**. They also include staff costs and depreciation provisions in respect of office furniture and equipment, in so far as these need not be shown under acquisition costs, claims incurred or investment charges.

3. ***Loss adjustment costs***: This item will encompass all expenses, internal or external, incurred directly or indirectly in respect of the management or adjustment of losses and claims. ***Direct expenses*** refer to all necessary expenditure for a company's claims department: salaries and wages paid to clerks, travel expenses (internal costs) and lawyers' fees and costs of legal proceedings (external expenditures). ***Indirect expenses*** refer to costs that cannot be allocated to individual claims: for example, a percentage of the rent to be allocated to the space occupied by the claims department or EDP costs for the settlement of claims. The provision for settlement costs is calculated without regard to the origin of claims.

4. ***Investment expenses:*** Three types of items are included in these expenses: *a)* investment management expenses; *b)* value adjustments on investments, *i.e.* adjustments for depreciation of fixed assets and for amortisation; *c)* losses on the realisation of investments. Under United States standards, they are broken down into: *a)* direct charges, which are usually external; *b)* direct assignment, which is internal and charged to investment activities; *c)* indirect allocation, which consists primarily of internal expenses and applies to more than a single expense group or function: for example, the salary of the company treasurer is charged to investment and accounting operations.

FINANCIAL (PRUDENTIAL) REGULATION

[*See also "OECD Insurance Guidelines" in the Annex, "Insurance Solvency Supervision (1995)" and "Policy Issues in Insurance (1993)".*]

Once an insurer is authorised to write insurance within a jurisdiction, consumer protection concerns drive governments to insist on certain continuing levels of insurer financial solidity. Insurance regulators are charged to oversee the continuing viability of insurers in the market through **financial regulation**, also referred to as **solvency regulation** and **prudential regulation**. Generally, the greater the detail and degree of financial **regulation**, the more secure the insurer. On the other hand, stringent oversight stifles competition and innovation and, thereby, can lower consumer value and choice. It is the government's difficult task to balance these competing public interests. With increasing liberalisation and deregulation, financial regulation becomes even more important.

If one aspect of solvency regulation must be singled out as the most critical, it would be an insurer's relative capital position. ***Capital*** is the excess of assets over liabilities. To gauge an insurer's capital, therefore, one must properly assess asset values and liability obligations.

If such an assessment is to be meaningful, insurers must follow similar procedures, for the terms "assets" and "liabilities" have meaning only in relation to some accounting convention. As a prerequisite to the establishment of acceptable levels of insurer financial solidity, governments therefore decide the acceptable **accounting principles** that insurers will be permitted or required to use.

Within the EU (and many other countries), minimum ongoing capital requirements are stated as the relationship between 1) capital and 2) **premiums** written (life and non-life), **claims incurred** (non-life), or **mathematical reserves** (life insurance). This required minimum relationship is called the ***solvency margin***. In addition to the solvency margin, a fixed minimum capital -- called the ***guaranty fund*** -- is also required. This amount generally is a lower, signalling threshold (one-third of the minimum solvency margin) and varies with the type of business. The solvency requirement in EU member states is the greater of the minimum solvency margin, which is volume dependent, and the minimum guaranty fund.

Within the United States, states' insurance laws have typically prescribed the same capital levels for newly licensed as for well-established insurers. These fixed amounts have had no necessary relationship to insurers' total policyholder obligations or to investment or other risks. In addition, regulators have used a variety of informal measures, including premiums-to-surplus ratios, to monitor insurer financial condition. Regulators are now using ***risk-based capital (RBC)*** standards, wherein minimum acceptable capital is directly related to the size and riskiness of a company's underwriting (technical) and investment (non-technical) operations. The system is fully operational in the United States (Similar systems exist in other countries. For example, in Canada with the "Minimum Continuing Capital and Surplus Requirements (MCCSR) and in Norway, where capital standards applicable to insurance companies are based on the same standards as those existing for banks).

The United States regulatory approach relies on a formula to derive the implied capital (the authorised control level) needed by an insurer to be able safely to carry the risk inherent in its assets, liabilities, and premium writings. The riskier the element, the larger the weighing factor and, hence, the larger the insurer's authorised control level (ACL).

The ACL is compared to the insurer's ***total adjusted capital*** (TA*C)* which is its statutory capital with adjustments for voluntary reserves and other items more properly classified as surplus. Values for this ratio determine whether government intervention is required. No regulatory action is required for ratios in excess of 200 per cent. Ratios between 150 and 200 per cent require the insurer to file an ***RBC Plan*** with the regulator. This plan is to describe the cause of the threat to the insurer's solvency, set out proposals for correction, give five years of financial projection, and provide other solvency-related information.

For RBC ratios between 100 and 150, the RBC Plan must be filed and the regulator must perform appropriate analysis and examinations of the insurer. Ratios between 70 and 100 subject the insurer to regulatory seizure. Ratios below 70 require regulatory seizure. (see **LIQUIDATION**)

The EU's approach is similar in concept. If a company's solvency margin falls below the prescribed minimum, a ***Recovery Plan*** must be filed with relevant authorities. The implementation of this medium-term plan is monitored to ensure that the insurer re-establishes its financial position. As in the United States, if the competent authorities believe that the company's financial position may deteriorate further, they may also restrict or prohibit the free disposal of assets by the company. In this case, they notify the authorities of the other member states in which the company is operating of all measures adopted so that these states can also take the same measures.

EU member states provide for a more aggressive approach for insurers whose solvency margins have fallen below the minimum guaranty fund. A ***Financial Plan*** must be provided to the competent authorities of the member state of origin. The short-term plan is to be submitted rapidly for approval to these authorities, which will monitor its implementation; the plan must propose measures for re-establishing the company's financial position, such as a call to shareholders, a merger with another company, etc.

To ensure solidity and investment diversification, governments generally establish quantitative and qualitative asset standards. Insurers are thereby prohibited or discouraged from undertaking what are considered imprudent investments or from failing to diversify their investments. Assets backing policyholder liabilities are routinely subject to more restrictive provisions than are assets backing capital and surplus or unassigned liabilities. High-risk illiquid investments are particularly limited.

Typical permissible investments include government-backed securities, corporate bonds, mortgage loans, common and preferred stock and real estate. Limitations ordinarily apply both as to quality and quantity for each asset category. For example, EU member states generally limit any one investment to 5 or 10 per cent of policyholder liabilities. Investments in foreign securities and illiquid or non-traded assets are restricted. An approach followed in a few countries (*e.g.*, Canada) that is gaining interest is to permit insurers broad investment discretion, subject to a ***"prudent person" rule***. This rule sets out general guidelines for acceptable investments. (see **INVESTMENT REGULATION**)

The appropriate valuation of an insurer's liabilities is critical to assessing its financial position. Life insurer policy reserves ordinarily are estimated through mathematical formulae whereas non-life insurer reserves are subject to less precise estimation methods. National laws are more general for non-life insurers' reserves.

Financial regulation can be considered as extending to insurer rehabilitation and **liquidation**. If an insurer must be liquidated with possible losses to policyholders, a governmentally run or sanctioned insolvency guaranty fund (**policyholder protection funds**) or other mechanism may be available to reduce policyholder losses, usually subject to some maximum payment per policyholder and possible loss sharing by the policyholder. [see **SOLVENCY RULES**]

FINANCIAL RESULTS

[*See also "Insurance Regulation and Supervision in Economies in Transition (1997)"*.]

Insurance company **financial results** are the means by which the financial effects of underwriting (technical) operations and investment and other (non-technical) operations are measured. Innumerable measures exist, the most general and most important of which is ***profit***, the difference between total income and the costs of production. A variation of profit is the ***operational result*** which is the difference between 1) **premiums** (defined in various ways) and investment income and 2) **claims incurred**, **expenses** and taxes. The ratio of (2) to (1) gives the ***operating ratio***. Insurers and reinsurers cannot succeed without favourable operational results over the long term.

The ***loss ratio*** is the ratio of incurred losses to net premiums earned for a period. ***Incurred losses*** (= **claims incurred**) equals paid losses, including loss adjustment expenses, plus the change in loss reserves for that period. ***Net premiums earned*** equals net premiums written plus the change in unearned premium reserves for that period. ***Net premiums written*** equals gross premiums written less **reinsurance** premiums ceded plus reinsurance premiums assumed. ***Gross premiums written*** equals total premium income from all direct insurance sold.

The ***expense ratio*** is the ratio of expenses incurred to net premiums written for a period, typically one year. (Some regulatory authorities use net premiums earned instead of net premiums written.) ***Expense incurred*** equals commissions, taxes, and underwriting, administrative and other expenses, except investment and losses adjustment expenses incurred, for that period.

The ***combined ratio***, another important measure of financial results, is the sum of the loss ratio and the expense ratio. The combined ratio is a measure of the underwriting (technical) results for a time period, typically one year. If the combined ratio is less than one, the insurer is said to have made an ***underwriting profit***.

The above and other measures of insurer financial results are important to numerous parties, including the insurance supervisor, **rating agencies**, current or potential investors, and policyholders. Insurance supervisors often use these measures calculated on a line-of-business basis in determining whether insurers are charging adequate or excessive rates. In countries with **rate regulation**, the supervisor will often be influenced by these measures in determining whether a requested rate change is justified.

FINANCIAL SERVICES CONGLOMERATES

[***Further information can be found in documentation produced by the "Joint Forum on Financial Conglomerates". The text below is illustrative only.***]

Following a definition used by the Joint Forum on Financial Conglomerates, a **financial services conglomerate** is a conglomerate whose primary business is financial, whose regulated entities engage to a significant extent in at least two of the activities of banking, insurance and securities business. ***Bancassurance*** describes the sale of insurance through banks, wherein insurers are primarily responsible for product manufacturing (production) and banks are primarily responsible for distribution. Regulations in most OECD countries do not allow ***cross production***, *e.g.* the underwriting of insurance by banks. In other words, only insurers may underwrite insurance products. But they allow ***cross distribution***, *e.g.* the selling of insurance products by banks. In order to do so, banks have used different strategies from alliances with traditional insurers to the most common one: creation of insurance subsidiaries. *Bancassurance* to date has mainly involved attempts by the traditional **distribution systems** of one institution to sell the products of another, mostly banks trying to sell insurance.

The trend toward financial services integration has led to several concerns by policy makers. The risk of ***contagion*** (financial infection) refers to the exposure (or damage) a tainted activity or component might inflict upon the financial service conglomerate. An **insurance company**, for example, may have a banking subsidiary that experiences enormous losses, and vice versa. The insurer might need to transfer significant amounts of capital to the bank, thereby placing the group as a whole at risk. At the same time, financial conglomeration should lead to greater diversification. If true, this fact theoretically should lower overall firm risk, not increase it.

Information disclosure and analysis by customers, intermediaries, **rating agencies** and governments have been suggested as a means of controlling the contagion exposure.

A related issue is **transparency,** which concerns the assurance that accurate information needed by customers, intermediaries, rating agencies and governments is readily available. Traditional financial measures of strength concentrate on balance sheets. As long as sufficient unrestricted capital remains to meet contingencies, organisations are deemed safe. Although this approach works reasonably well when institutions remain within sectoral boundaries and like institutions are roughly comparable, financial conglomeration requires a broader consideration of factors.

Another policy issue relates to ***management responsibility***, which concerns the possibility that managers might compromise their entity's sound operation in favour of the conglomerate's fiscal health (*e.g.*, through unwise loans to connected parties). Where a financial services group is regulated functionally, how can each sector's regulator be assured that managers will fulfil their responsibility to meet regulatory requirements given other interests within the group? Although there are serious analysis and enforcement limitations on regulatory agencies, some believe the solution is to include a broad obligation to disclose major intra-group transactions. Disclosure could entail transactions that affect the regulated entity or the basic integrity of the regulated unit's assets and operating capacity. At a minimum, these data should constitute a prerequisite for continuing authority to operate.

Double-gearing exists when a company includes the capital of subsidiaries to meet its own solvency requirements. This double counting acts to inflate the conglomerate's apparent capital. Clear, uniform accounting standards and requirements are necessary to identify double-gearing. Issues related to appropriate disclosure and the appropriate locus of regulatory responsibility must be resolved.

Market power relates to the ability of one or a few sectoral dominant firms (*e.g.*, through oligopoly or monopoly) to influence market prices. A highly concentrated market or the existence of vertical agreements may lead to market power which hinders market efficiency. Countries rely on **competition regulation**, among other regulatory tools, to curtail such risk.

The potential for ***conflict of interest*** exists when a financial institution offers multiple financial services and promotes proprietary products through coercion or other power for the organisation's benefit over the best interest of the customer. Some have argued that banks should not be permitted to sell insurance because they may condition the availability of other products on the customer's agreement to purchase insurance.

Most financial services regulatory systems prohibit tying the purchase of one product to another, although discounts are permitted for joint purchase. As with prior points, some believe information disclosure and competitor exploitation of potential abuses may avoid such conflicts. A final regulatory concern is ***regulatory arbitrage*** which is the tendency of financial service conglomerates to shift activities or positions within the group to avoid certain regulation in whole or in part. For example, a conglomerate might shift the production and sale of a particular savings product to its insurance company if insurance regulation was judged less intrusive than banking regulation. Lacking comprehensive cross-sector and international regulatory harmonisation, opportunities for such arbitrage probably will always exist. It has been suggested that, to control this practice, sectoral regulators should engage in extensive cross-sector information sharing. Internationally, regulators of multinational financial services firms could also engage in informational reciprocity. The possibility of regulatory arbitrage encourages cross-sectoral and international regulatory harmonisation.

INSURANCE COMPANY

An **insurance company** or **insurer** is any organisation that issues insurance policies and that bears insurance risk. The two most prevalent forms of insurers world-wide are stocks and mutuals. ***Stock insurers*** are owned by shareholders, with profits accruing to them. ***Mutual insurers*** have no shareholders, being owned by and profits flowing to policyholders. The stock insurer form predominates in most lines and markets world-wide. Mutuals control important market shares in several countries, especially in **life insurance**. (see **DEMUTUALISATION**)

Insurers that sell insurance to the public and to non-insurance commercial and industrial enterprises are called ***direct writing*** (or ***primary***) ***insurers*** (and attendant premiums are ***direct written premiums***). Insurers that sell insurance to direct writing insurers to hedge their own insurance portfolios are called ***reinsurers***. Direct writing companies purchase **reinsurance** to avoid undue potential loss concentrations, to secure greater underwriting capacity, to stabilise overall financial results and to take advantage of special expertise of the reinsurer. As the direct writing company ordinarily is a knowledgeable buyer and the reinsurer is a knowledgeable seller, government intervention into the transaction has historically been non-existent or kept to a minimum. Reinsurance is probably the most international segment of the insurance business.

Thousands of businesses world-wide are involved in various sophisticated self-insurance programs. ***Captive insurers*** are insurance companies created and owned by a firm or group of firms primarily for purposes of insuring the firm or group. These non-traditional self-funding approaches may account for as much as one-third of United States commercial **non-life insurance** direct written **premiums**, and the proportion is growing. They account for a smaller but growing presence in other countries' markets. For tax and regulatory reasons, most captive insurers are not domiciled in the parent company's jurisdiction. Insurance placed with captives technically is cross-border insurance. (see **CROSS-BORDER INSURANCE TRADE**)

National insurance markets typically are composed of some combination of domestic and foreign insurers -- or at least foreign-owned insurers. A ***domestic insurer*** is one domiciled (incorporated) in the same jurisdiction in which it is authorised to sell insurance, ordinarily the jurisdiction is the concerned country, except in the United States where it is the United States state in which the insurer is domiciled. A ***foreign insurer*** is one doing business in a jurisdiction in which it is not domiciled. Ordinarily the jurisdiction is another country except in the United States where the term refers to an insurer domiciled in another US state. In the United States, an insurer domiciled in another country is called an ***alien insurer***. Ordinarily a foreign insurer must become an ***authorised insurer*** to do business within another jurisdiction. (see **AUTHORISATION**)

INVESTMENT REGULATIONS

[See also "OECD Insurance Guidelines" in the Annex and "Policy Issues in Insurance (1996)".]

(Remark: the item is dealt with here very briefly and in an illustrative manner, as the issues it covers are treated in various other items. The reader is also invited to refer to the publication on "Insurance Regulation and Supervision in OECD Countries (1999)".)

Four distinct purposes are often mentioned for the **regulation** of the investment policies of **insurance companies**.

1. The main purpose is related to the protection of policyholders (consumers): Constraints on the investment choice of insurers exist as part of the wider aim of seeking to minimise the probability that insurers go bankrupt and to ensure that the costs to policyholders are kept to a minimum, if it does occur. Because consumers pay **premiums** to insurers in advance, how these funds are invested before they receive their contingent payments is naturally a relevant supervisory concern. This concern tends to be greater for **life insurance** than for **non-life insurance**, because of the longer term nature of the life insurance contracts, because the size of invested funds is larger and because the funds represent to a significant degree the long term saving of the public.

2. Protection of financial stability of thc insurance company and the economy as a whole: Insurance companies are indeed the biggest institutional investors in OECD area. Adverse investment strategy may lead to the emergence of financial crisis. Even in the case of bankruptcy of limited number of companies, taxpayers may have to contribute if **policyholder protection funds** are not sufficiently funded.

3. Directing the flow of investable funds: Since insurance companies, especially life insurers, control a sizeable proportion of the stock and flow of long-term personal savings in many developed economies, governments sometimes feel that they would like to influence the direction of these stocks and flows in the pursuit of their wider economic goals.

4. Reducing a potential concentration of power within the financial sector: In some OECD countries, governments have historically tried to put limits on the diversification strategies of insurance companies

in order to prevent them using their considerable financial resources to control other financial institutions. In most countries, however, the supervisory authorities have allowed insurance institutions to bypass these restrictions through the use of non-insurance holding company structures.

Insurance acts or statutes are the principle method by which investment policies of insurance companies are regulated. The primary concern of such insurance legislation is the protection of policyholders. These statutes are now generally promulgated at the national or federal level. Constraints on the investment choice of insurance companies imposed by insurance legislation can be characterised as having one or more of the following aims:

- Financial assets which are held should possess acceptably low levels of default risk;

- Investment portfolio should be adequately diversified so that default risk is further reduced and there is sufficient liquidity to cover potential short-term cash flow needs (see **SPREAD AND DIVERSIFICATION OF INVESTMENT**);

- The composition of investment portfolios should be sufficiently matched to the nature of liabilities so that there is a high probability that the contractual payments to policyholders will be met. (see **MATCHING RULES**)

- Restrictions should be placed on the localisation or physical custody of investments. This regulatory concern is not only to ensure proof of ownership, which is particularly important in countries with a tradition for issuing bearer securities, but also with minimising the potential for fraud by company management. (see **LOCALISATION OF ASSETS**)

In all OECD countries, there are approved lists of financial assets, viz. admissible assets, in which the funds applicable to policyholders' liabilities (**technical provisions**) can be invested. Approved investments (often called ***admissible investments***) are deemed to have acceptable default risk and other desirable investment risk characteristics. These lists are found within the insurance legislation, although there are sometimes powers given to a regulatory authority so that they can be changed if it is thought necessary. Some lists are less restrictive than others, depending on the degree of liberality of the regulation tradition in the country and on the range of investment opportunities that exist in the local capital market. Such approved lists are detailed to ensure that investments which insurers hold possess acceptable levels of default risk and other investment risk characteristics, especially liquidity. Liquidity of an investment has two interrelated aspects: price or value stability and marketability. Both of these aspects of liquidity are necessary if an insurance company is to be able to sell investments at short notice in order to meet its contractual obligations to policyholders, with any high degree of certainty that the intrinsic value of investments will be realised.

The same requirement may also be extended to the assets held against the minimum statutory capital, other reserves and the free capital. Alternatively these assets held against the minimum statutory capital may be subject to less restrictive requirements and the investment of the free capital may be subject to no constraints at all. In this respect, OECD's Insurance Guidelines for Economies in Transition mentions that:

"At this stage, regulatory and supervisory authorities should make sure that a distinction applies between the treatment of investments representing technical reserves and that of investments of the capital base. The latter has a role to play in the long run, particularly with respect to the funding of the company's future growth, and it would be sound policy to let companies earn a high return on the investment of their capital base, so that they may reinforce their financial resources. However, the buffer effect of the capital base in its role as a complement to technical provisions and possible **equalisation reserves** may serve as grounds for justifying restrictions placed on investments of these funds. Thus, one will also have to distinguish, within owners' equity itself, between the minimum required capital and the free capital. While there is a need for regulations on the investment of the minimum capital - which ought to be readily available to pay exceptionally high claims - those concerning the investment of the free capital seem less justified."

Recent trends in regulation of investment highlight the need:

- to match further this regulation with regulation of liabilities and

- to consider both institutional and functional approach.

Important debates are also ongoing in OECD countries on "quantitative" versus ***"prudent person" approaches***, which relies more on "industry" mechanisms and reflects deregulation trends. It is finally very important to underline the significance of valuation methods on the actual impact of investment regulations.

LIFE INSURANCE (ASSURANCE)

In the narrowest sense, **life insurance (assurance)** is any form of insurance whose payment is contingent upon whether the insured is dead (or alive). In a broader sense, it extends to any form of insurance whose payment is contingent on the insured's health. (When used in this more general form, the term ***personal insurance*** is commonly used outside the United States.) In this broad sense, the life branch includes insurance that pays benefits on a person's 1) death (usually called life insurance or assurance), 2) living a certain period (endowments, annuities and pensions), 3) disability (disability insurance) and 4) injury or incurring a disease (health insurance). In some markets, notably in Europe, health insurance is more commonly classified as **non-life insurance**. This is also the case with the insurance statistics compiled by the OECD.

The insurance business has historically divided itself between companies that sell life insurance and those that sell non-life insurance. The life and non-life branches perceive themselves quite differently, and with some justification. Life insurance policies generally pose a greater challenge for the customer than do non-life policies because premium payments may span many years and policies often build non-guaranteed cash values which makes their evaluation more complex. Most OECD countries require life and non-life products to be underwritten by different companies or at least to be managed separately.

Some countries permit, however, a single insurer (***composite insurer***) to sell both types of insurance or the law prohibiting creation of composite insurers have grandfathered companies already operating at the time of passage, but usually with management restrictions.

The two generic forms of death-based life insurance are term and whole life insurance. ***Term life insurance*** pays a set amount to the beneficiary if the insured dies within the policy term. If the insured survives the policy term, the policy expires without value or payment. ***Whole life insurance*** pays a set amount to the beneficiary whenever the insured dies. Ordinarily, whole life insurance policies carry level premiums which lead to cash values within the policy. If the policyholder voluntarily terminates the policy, the cash value is paid.

Two generic forms of life insurance pay if the insured survives: endowment and life annuities. ***Endowment insurance*** pays a set amount to the insured if he or she survives the policy term or, commonly, to the beneficiary if the insured dies during the policy term. A ***life annuity*** pays an amount periodically (*e.g.*, monthly) to the insured (annuitant) if he or she is alive at the end of each period.

Variations of the above forms include variable life insurance and universal life insurance. ***Variable (unit linked) life insurance*** is any form of whole life or endowment insurance whose reserves and cash values are backed by and directly linked to a portfolio of securities. ***Universal life insurance*** is any form of life insurance that carries no fixed premiums, whose internal operation is transparent and whose death benefit is adjustable.

Life insurance is often classified by whether it is sold to a group of persons, such as employees of a single employer (***group insurance*** or ***pensions***), or to individuals (commonly referred to as ***ordinary insurance*** or ***individual pensions***). Both group and individual forms of disability and health insurance exist in most markets.

Because of the complexity of the life insurance purchase, some countries set out elaborate marketing rules. Such rules may require the intermediary to prove that he or she has given best advice, knows the customer and has recommended a policy suitable for the individual's circumstances. Certain policy disclosure, sometimes including intermediary compensation, is typically required as well. Prohibitions on the use of certain terminology may be set out, along with the required use of other terminology.

Because some life insurance policies involve substantial, long-term consumer savings and not only a promise to pay a claim, life insurers are often considered important financial intermediaries in a country's financial system. Their failure could have significant repercussions, not only with insurers' customers who have entrusted their savings to them, but also potentially for confidence in a nation's financial system.

LIFE INSURANCE PROVISION (MATHEMATICAL PROVISION OR RESERVE)

In **life insurance**, **technical provisions** are equal to the actuarial value of the insurer's commitments in respect of:

- guaranteed benefits;
- declared bonuses;
- options offered;
- corporate **expenses**; net of:
- the actuarial value of future **premiums**, which may be reduced for management loading.

Such provisions must generally be computed separately for each contract, on the basis of projections that take into account:

- a margin for unfavourable variations in the various relevant factors;
- the method of valuing representative assets on the basis of their market value or acquisition cost;
- a prudent interest rate, depending on:
  - the type of contract, with or without bonuses;
  - guaranteed income or contract linked to an accounting unit;
  - the currency in which commitments are denominated;
  - the corresponding representative assets.

This provision must be supplemented in order to cover interest-rate commitments to policyholders if the current or foreseeable return on assets is insufficient to meet those commitments. It may include the provision for ***deferred premiums***, corresponding to the proportion of gross premiums to be allocated to the following financial year or to subsequent years; alternatively, that provision can be shown as a separate item (***provision for unearned premiums***). The deferred acquisition costs corresponding to these premiums can be shown explicitly on the balance sheet as an asset or deducted from the relevant liability.

LIQUIDATION

[*See also "OECD Insurance Guidelines" in the Annex, "Policy Issues in Insurance (1996)" and "Insurance Solvency Supervision (1995)".*]

When recovery measures (see ***recovery plan***) have been unsuccessful or are impossible to implement, the supervisor may have to put the company in severe difficulties in suspension, termination or liquidation process. (see **SUSPENSION AND TERMINATION**)

The ability to place an insurer in **liquidation** (or rehabilitation, where available) varies from one country to another. Some jurisdictions, such as France, give only the insurance regulator that power. Others, such as Sweden and Germany, require the board of directors to report insolvency to the regulator, with Germany providing a penalty of up to three years in prison for failure to do so. However, others, such as the United Kingdom and Japan, generally follow the corporate bankruptcy scheme which grants the power to all interested parties. For example, in the United Kingdom, a petition for liquidation may be filed by the company, its directors, one or more creditors or contributories, and ten or more policyholders. In the United States, neither creditors nor policyholders have the right to petition for the liquidation of an insurer. In Japan, the auditor, among others, who is a mandatory member of the board, may petition for liquidation of the company.

For illustration, readers will find below the specific procedures followed in France, Germany, the United Kingdom, and the United States.

France

French insurer insolvency law has no provisions for a liquidation proceeding to be initiated by the debtor or any creditors. It is up to the Ministry of Economy and Finances and to the Commission to decide whether an insurer should be liquidated.
As soon as an insurer's solvency begins to deteriorate, the Commission implements recovery and safeguard procedures. In case of failure of an insurer, the Minister withdraws the company's **authorisation**, which, under the French Insurance Code, involves the liquidation of the insurance company.

1. A liquidator appointed by the Chief Justice at the Commission's request will be in charge of administering and liquidating the insurer's assets.

2. As from the date a liquidator is appointed, individual lawsuits by creditors are suspended.

3. A six-month report is sent to the judge-commissioner on the state of the winding-up.

4. An official receiver appointed by the Chief Justice will supervise the liquidation.

5. The liquidator will receive the creditors' claims one month after the withdrawal order.

6. Claims not reported to the Court within the prescribed period, and disputed claims, will not be included in the distribution of funds unless approved.

7. The liquidator will pay creditors' claims according to their ranking.

French common law is very seldom applicable (to the liquidation of an insurance company) because most assets have already been exhausted after insurance liquidation proceedings.

Germany

In case of insolvency or excessive indebtedness, the board of directors of the insurer must inform the supervisory authority, BAV (Bundesaufsichtsamt für das Versicherungswesen) accordingly. If, after close examination of the insurer, the BAV judges that bankruptcy can be avoided, the BAV will take all necessary measures such as prohibition of payments or reduction of benefits in case of **life insurance**. To prevent any restoration measures from being endangered by third parties, only the BAV is entitled to file a petition for bankruptcy. If the BAV decides to file this motion, it must be filed in the court of bankruptcy having jurisdiction where the insurer's head office is located. The court of bankruptcy will then issue an order of bankruptcy. From that time on, a court appointed liquidator assumes complete authority and winds up the company according to the provisions in the Insolvency Code. The insurer has the right to appeal.

United Kingdom

In the United Kingdom, the procedure for liquidating any insolvent company, be it an insurance company or not, and distributing its assets to the company creditors is known as a ***winding-up***.

The basic legislation is the Insurance Companies Act, which stipulates that **insurance companies** may be liquidated under the Insolvency Act of 1986, but for **reinsurance** no specific text is applicable.

A winding-up may be either voluntary or initiated by the court (compulsory).

1. Compulsory liquidations

The most common ground on which a company is compulsorily wound up is that it is unable to pay its debts. However, compulsory liquidations may be initiated on the basis of a court determination that liquidation is just and equitable. A petition for an order of liquidation may be presented to the court either by the company, its directors, creditors or contributories , ten or more policyholders owing policies of an aggregate value of not less than ten thousand pounds Sterling, or the Secretary of State.

Upon the issuance of a winding-up order, the Official Receiver is automatically appointed liquidator, who may convene a meeting of creditors to appoint another liquidator and also a liquidation committee to oversee the liquidator. If the liquidator believes the interests of the company's creditors attributable to its long-term business require the appointment of a special manager of such business, the liquidator may apply to the court for an order appointing a special manager with such powers as the court may direct.

2. *Voluntary liquidations*

Two types of voluntary liquidations exist, those of members and those of creditors.

In a member's voluntary liquidation, if the directors of a company determine that it would be impossible to avoid winding-up, then they may voluntarily liquidate the company. The directors must make a declaration of solvency that all debts will be paid in full within a stipulated period of time not exceeding twelve months. The time scale makes a members voluntary liquidation unlikely for a solvent insurance company.

In a creditor's voluntary liquidation, the shareholders resolve to place the company into voluntary liquidation and appoint a liquidator. Financial information relating to the company is produced at a meeting of creditors. The creditors also appoint a liquidator at this meeting. If the two are different, the creditors' nominee is appointed. The shareholders maintain a right to appeal to the court. The creditors may also appoint a liquidation committee, with the members retaining the right to make appointment.

Insurers carrying on long-term (life) insurance business within the United Kingdom may not be voluntarily liquidated. Unless the court orders otherwise, the liquidator shall carry on the long-term business of an insurer "with the view to its being transferred as a going concern to another insurance company, whether an existing company or a company formed for that purpose." Policyholders of the United Kingdom are characterised more as creditors of the insurance corporation on a footing similar to other creditors, rather than beneficiaries of a fiduciary relationship as is common in the United States.

United States

In the United States, the laws of the individual states govern insurance company insolvencies. There is no national or federal insurance law. However, recognising the likelihood of interstate insurer insolvencies and the desirability for a uniform means of regulating the conservation and liquidation of the assets of insolvent insurers, two model insolvency administration acts have been developed. The acts are known as the Insurers Rehabilitation and Liquidation Model Act (the Model Act), developed by the National Association of Insurance Commissioners (NAIC), and the Uniform Insurers Liquidation Act (the UILA), developed by the National Conference of Commissioners on Uniform State Laws, and one of them has been adopted in some form in almost all of the states. Being more comprehensive than the UILA, the Model Act has been adopted in the majority of the states. While there are variations in the treatment of insolvent insurers among the several states even where the Model Act has been adopted, the difference are generally not significant.

In the United States, only the insurance Commissioner of a state may commence delinquency proceedings against an insurer. There are two types of delinquency proceedings under the Model Act:

1. ***Rehabilitation proceedings***: the Model Act requires that the Commissioner petition the proper court for an order authorising him to place an insolvent insurer into rehabilitation. To obtain such an order, the Commissioner must demonstrate a compelling reason to place the insurer under his control. The order of rehabilitation appoints the Commissioner as the rehabilitator and directs the rehabilitator to take immediate possession of the assets of the insurer and to administer them under the general supervision of the court. If the rehabilitator determines that the insurer is likely to be successful, he may prepare and submit to the court a plan of reorganisation, consolidation, conversion, reinsurance, merger or other transformation. At such time as the Commissioner deems appropriate, he may petition the court for an order that the rehabilitation has been accomplished and the property be restored to the insurer. Conversely, if the Commissioner's attempts as rehabilitation are unsuccessful, he may petition the court for an order of liquidation. (see also ***recovery plan***)

2. ***Liquidation proceedings***: the grounds for obtaining a liquidation order include all grounds upon which the Commissioner may seek a rehabilitation order; a finding that the insurer is insolvent; or the Commissioner's belief that further transaction of business by the insurer would be hazardous to policyholders, creditors, or the public. An order of liquidation is substantially similar to an order of rehabilitation, except that the date the order is issued fixes the right and liabilities of the insurer and of the insurer's creditors, policyholders, shareholders or members and other interested persons and directs the receiver to give notice of the liquidation to all interested parties, marshal the assets of the insolvent insurer, and ultimately make distributions to creditors in accordance with a prescribed priority of distribution.

[see **FINANCIAL (PRUDENTIAL) REGULATION**]

LOCALISATION OF ASSETS

[*See also "OECD Insurance Guidelines" in the Annex and "Policy Issues in Insurance (1996)".*]

Apart form the constraints on the investment choices of insurance companies, it is common for national legislation to place restrictions on the localisation or physical custody of investments. This regulatory concern is not just to ensure proof of ownership, which is particularly important in countries with a tradition for issuing bearer securities, but also with minimising the potential for fraud by company management. This custody role can be undertaken by **insurance company** itself, but it is more usual for the securities, and associated ownership documentation, to be required to be held in trust by an approved bank or trust company.

Most OECD countries require insurers to physically hold assets corresponding to the **technical provisions** within the country. In the EU and EEA markets, this localisation concept is extended to different countries within the area.

In the EU, **localisation of assets** means the existence of assets, whether movable or immovable, within a Member State, but it is not construed as requiring that movable property be deposited or that immovable property be subject to restrictive measures such as the registration of mortgages. Assets representing claims against debtors should be situated in the Member State where they are to be liquidated.

An EU Member State may allow technical provisions to be covered by claims against reinsurers and fix the percentage of the allowance, but it may not specify the location of such claims. Agencies or branches of non-EU undertakings operating within the EU are subject to the requirement that assets totalling at least the amount of the minimum guaranty fund must be located in the country of operation and that an initial deposit of one-quarter of those assets must be made as security. Such non-EU establishments must also possess, in the country of operation, free assets equal to the amount of the guaranty fund, net of intangible items, to cover a solvency margin which is computed with reference to premiums and claims corresponding exclusively to such operations. The portion exceeding minimum free assets may be located in other Member States.

Non-EU undertakings that have been authorised in several Members States have their solvency assessed on an overall basis, once all of the Member States to which application was made have given their joint consent. Assessment will be carried out by the competent authorities of the Member State chosen by the undertaking, which must state the reasons for its choice. The advantages of overall assessment are as follows:

1. The solvency margin is calculated on the basis of aggregate business in the EU.

2. The required guaranty is deposited in one chosen Member State.

3. The assets covering the guaranty fund may be deposited in any of the Member States.

(see **INVESTMENT REGULATIONS**)

MARKET ACCESS

[See also "OECD Insurance Guidelines" in the Annex and "Liberalisation of International Insurance Operations (1999)".]

A right of **market access** is a fair-trade principle meaning that foreign firms should have a right to enter a country's market. Access can be via **establishment** or **cross-border**, with the mode giving rise to different public policy considerations.

A right of market access is fundamental to the principle of free trade, yet no country permits foreign insurers completely unrestrained market access. This is because of the potential for consumer abuse that exists were no market entry standards imposed.

Free-trade advocates acknowledge the need for protecting consumers from possible harm that could arise from unbridled foreign insurer market access. At the same time, they note that many countries impose entry barriers that are seemingly unrelated to consumer protection concerns.

The extreme in market access denial occurs in countries with monopolist insurers. Other countries may flatly deny access to all foreign insurers or do so somewhat more indirectly through ***localisation of ownership*** rules that require the majority if not the totality of insurer ownership to be held by nationals of the country. Countries often also have ***domestication requirements*** under which foreign insurers are permitted to conduct business within a market only via local establishment of a subsidiary. A domestication requirement is often coupled with a requirement for ***localisation of insurance***, meaning that certain or all lines of insurance covering property or lives situated within a country or liability related thereto must be placed with locally licensed insurers only. A common variation of the localisation of insurance requirement, often found in developing countries, is a regulation or law that insists that imports (and sometimes exports) must be insured in the local market.

Some countries limit market access through stipulations that foreign insurers may not conduct operations unless their products are unavailable locally or unless their operations are judged by local authorities to result in substantial benefit to the local economy -- a so-called ***needs test***.

Finally, market access is limited when governments impose mandatory cessions. ***Mandatory cessions*** are requirements that national insurers must reinsure certain portions of their direct business with national or regional reinsurers. Their purpose is to increase local retention capacity and to be able to negotiate better **reinsurance** terms internationally with a much larger volume of premiums than would be the case of individual negotiations by a single local insurer. Their effect is to limit other reinsurers' access to the national reinsurance market.

MATCHING RULES

[***See also "OECD Insurance Guidelines" in the Annex and "Policy Issues in Insurance (1996)".***]

One important area of **investment regulation** is the extent to which there are explicit requirements to match assets (*i.e.* investments) to policyholder liabilities (*i.e.* **technical provisions**). This is because one aspect of risk for an **insurance company** is the mismatch of assets and liabilities. (see **RISKS FACED BY INSURANCE COMPANIES**) There are two main aspects of matching that one might expect to find within national insurance legislation. One relates to the matching of the maturity or duration profiles of investments with those of the policyholder liabilities (***maturity matching***). The other is concerned with the extent to which an insurance company holds investments in the same currencies as its liabilities (***currency matching***).

1. Maturity matching

Since the nature of the liabilities of a **non-life insurance** company and those of a **life insurance** company are quite different, one might expect the investment regulations to reflect these differences, as investments covering technical provisions for non-life insurance can, in principle, differ from those for life insurance. With respect to non-life, where the nature of policyholder liabilities are mainly short-term and claim payments are unpredictable in their size and timing, a suitably matched investment portfolio is one that possesses a high degree of liquidity, *i.e.* low price volatility and good marketability. Life insurance (and annuity) liabilities are different, since they tend to have a much longer maturity and often contain implicit interest rate guarantees. One of the main investment risks for a life insurance company is to ensure that the duration of its investments is broadly in line with those of its liabilities, in order to minimise this inherent interest rate risk. In the main, interest rate risk arises if investments are held too short such that interest rates may fall and remain low when funds require reinvestment. In addition, for life contracts with a significant savings component, there is a competitive, if not a legal, requirement to ensure that the rates of return on investment holdings maintain their value in real terms, *i.e.* keep up with local inflation.

Hence one might expect that within the **regulations** governing life insurance investment, there may well be some requirements to ensure that the duration or maturity profile of investments tend to match to those of technical provisions. Recent works in this respect are promoting the development of assets/liabilities management techniques. At the same time one must recognise that to set down clear rules relating to a complex financial characteristic such as duration, or a general framework such as immunisation, may be so difficult as to discourage any attempt to formalise them within a legislative framework. But any lack of formal rules should not necessarily mean that no regard is paid by a regulatory authority to maturity matching considerations. This might be done on an informal basis as a part of the wider assessment of the solvency of an insurance company. (see **FINANCIAL (PRUDENTIAL) REGULATION**)

2. Currency matching

The second area of matching regulations pertains to currency risk. A prudent policy for an insurance company is to hold investments in those currencies in which it expects future payments to policyholders to arise. If an insurer holds investments in currencies other than those in which the liabilities are likely to be paid in the future, there is the possibility that the currency in which the investments are held might have depreciated by the time claims have to be paid. A large currency loss could clearly jeopardise the financial viability of an insurance company. But it is only at the time that the claims need to be paid that a currency risk to the insurer actually arises. However, since there is uncertainty about the timing of claim payments, particularly in non-life insurance, prudence suggests that investments should be held in a matched currency position over the duration of the run-off period of the liabilities, since payments to policyholders might be needed earlier than anticipated.

There is the issue of whether currency matching rules should relate just to those investments covering technical provisions or should extend to the investment of the capital base. There is a good case for requiring insurance companies to currency match the investments covering their technical provisions, especially in an economic environment of floating exchange rates, but there is less of a case to require the currency matching of the capital base. In practice, insurers would seek to invest some of their capital base in a mix of currencies especially if they are undertaking international business, but not necessarily precisely in those currencies in which their policyholder liabilities are likely to arise. This is because an insurance company will wish to insulate itself against the financial impact on its capital base of a sharp fall in a single currency, including its domestic currency, caused by a major economic or political shock or large natural catastrophe. But the case for a statutory requirement to currency match the funds covering the capital base is not a strong one, particularly as these funds often belong to shareholders.

This issue of currency matching is separate from the investment regulations relating to foreign investment. Restrictions on foreign investment tend to be concerned primarily with default and liquidity risk considerations. However, they can be used to indirectly control any significant degree of currency mismatching. Within the EU, there is a general philosophy that separate regulations for currency matching should exist and not be embodied within more general restrictions on foreign investment, not least because of a wider economic aim of free capital movements.

Within the EU, up to 20 per cent of liabilities in a given currency may be covered by non-matching assets. EU Member States may waive the matching principles in the following cases:

1. If application of the principle would result in the company's head office or a branch office being obliged to hold assets in a currency amounting to not more than 7 per cent of the assets existing in other currencies;

2. If liabilities are payable in a non-EU currency:

- if investments in that currency are regulated;
- if the currency is subject to transfer restrictions;
- or not suitable for covering technical provisions.

Moreover, with the introduction of the Euro, there is now even greater investment flexibility for insurers in the Euro-zone countries, whereby 100 % of investments can be held in the Euro or in other Euro-zone national currencies against liabilities denominated in any of those currencies.

NATIONAL TREATMENT

[*See also "OECD Insurance Guidelines" in the Annex* **and** *"Liberalisation of International Insurance Operations (1999)".*]

The fair-trade principle of **national treatment** requires governments to enact and administer domestic laws and **regulations** such that foreign products and services are accorded treatment no less favourable than that which is accorded to domestic producers in similar circumstances. National treatment can be thought of as a type of **non-discrimination** standard applied to domestic operations, after **market access** is secured. It is intended to ensure equality of competitive opportunity for foreign entrants.

National treatment problems exist for foreign insurers in some markets. Thus, some countries have different deposit or capital requirements for foreign insurers than for domestic ones. Many countries assess higher taxes on foreign insurers than on domestic insurers. Some countries deny or restrict foreign insurer membership in local trade associations, thus denying them equivalent access to domestic statistics, research and lobbying.

Denial of equality of competitive opportunity can take on more subtle forms. For example, countries that strictly regulate product prices and forms and that prohibit use of certain distribution techniques (*e.g.*, independent agents, **brokers** or direct response) may not be violating a strict interpretation of the national treatment standard, but their actions constitute hindrances to new entrants. Such strict regulation affords already established firms a competitive advantage over new entrants, whether foreign or domestic.

NON-DISCRIMINATION

[***See also "OECD Insurance Guidelines" in the Annex and "Liberalisation of International Insurance Operations (1999)"***]

Non-discrimination, also known as **most-favoured-nation (MFN) treatment**, is a fair-trade principle meaning that no country's firms obtain more favourable market access than any other country's firms. Thus, an MFN trading partner's businesses enjoy the best possible (*i.e.*, the *most* favourable) market access.

In combination with **reciprocity**, non-discrimination can lead to dramatic liberalisation. Suppose country A is willing to lower its tariffs (because of reciprocity) to gain access to country B's market. If a deal can be made, non-discrimination requires that both country A and B lower their tariffs for all of their MFN trading partners, not just with respect to each other. These actions can spark another round of tariff cutting as other parties reciprocate.

If two large economies strike a certain liberalised market access bargain toward each other, the MFN principle requires the same bargain to be extended to small economies as well -- economies that may not enjoy much bargaining clout. By a combination of these principles, a little trade liberalisation can be expanded and increased.

MFN says nothing about whether market access is granted or about the nature of that access. It addresses only the narrow element of whether the host country treats foreigners similarly, which can mean that the country treats all foreigners equally poorly or well and still be consistent with the MFN principle. Thus, a country that prevents all foreign insurers from entering its market would be treating all foreign firms equally.

NON-LIFE INSURANCE

Non-life insurance is any form of insurance not defined as **life insurance** and includes insurance to cover 1) property losses (*i.e.*, damage to or destruction of homes, automobiles, businesses, aircraft, ships, etc.; 2) liability losses (*i.e.*, payments due to professional negligence, product defects, negligent automobile operation, etc.); and, in some countries, 3) workers' compensation (and health insurance) payments. This branch of insurance is often referred to as **property/casualty insurance**, **property and liability insurance** or **general insurance**.

Non-life insurance purchased by individuals (*e.g.*, homeowners insurance, automobile insurance, etc.) is classified as ***personal lines insurance***. Within the EU, such insurances (plus that for small businesses) are generally referred to as insurance for ***mass risks***. Non-life insurance purchased by businesses and other organisations (*e.g.*, product liability, business interruption, automobile insurance, etc.) is classified as ***commercial lines insurance***. Within the EU, such insurances (except for small businesses) are generally called insurance for ***large risks***. In some markets, insurance purchased by commercial organisations, especially manufacturing firms, is termed ***industrial insurance***. Marine, aviation and transport (MAT) insurances are considered commercial lines.

Government oversight is more stringent in the personal than in the commercial lines because of greater information asymmetry problems in personal lines; *i.e.*, individual customers are less knowledgeable than commercial customers. **Rate regulation** is more common in the non-life branch than in the life branch and, within the non-life branch, is more common in personal lines than in commercial lines.

OTHER NON-LIFE PROVISIONS

In addition to the non-life provisions separately dealt with as main terms (*), the following provisions might be worth mentioning:

1. ***mathematical provision for annuities***: This provision covers remaining annuity payments at the valuation date. It is used in Belgium, Denmark, France, Germany and the Netherlands.

2. ***provision for premium refunds***: This provision is set aside at the valuation date to adjust the insurer's commitments as a result of a reduction or elimination of risks. It exists in Germany and also in France, where it includes the provision for suspended risks.

3. ***provision for risk of non-availability of investment***: This is a provision set aside in France when the aggregate book value of investments other than securities subject to depreciation exceeds the probable realisation value thereof.

4. ***provision for return premiums***: This is a provision for the probable depreciation of premiums receivable from policyholders at the last day of the accounting year. It exists in Spain, where it is considered a technical provision.

5. ***provision for risks specific to large aircraft***: This provision is to offset risks inherent to jumbo aircraft.

6. ***provision to cover pay-outs in the form of a draw***: This provision is specific to companies operating funded schemes with draws for policyholders. It exists only in Spain.

(* see **PROVISION FOR THE AGEING OF RISKS, PROVISION FOR UNEARNED PREMIUMS, PROVISION FOR UNEXPIRED RISKS AND PROVISION FOR OUTSTANDING CLAIMS**)

POLICYHOLDER PROTECTION FUNDS (INSURANCE GUARANTY FUNDS)

[*See also "OECD Insurance Guidelines" in the Annex, "Insurance Regulation and Supervision in OECD Countries (1999)" and "Insurance Solvency Supervision (1995)".*]

In most of the OECD Member countries, at least one "fund" or "scheme" exists for the purpose of protecting certain policyholders of **insurance companies** that are either in financial difficulty or insolvent and consequently unable to meet their liabilities. Such funds are normally established under the relevant insurance laws and are usually financed by contributions from participating insurers in proportion to their respective annual **premium** income from the business being protected.

Such funds can be broken down into the following types:

1. ***Funds for a specific class of insurance***: *i.e.*, funds covering only one specific branch, typically motor vehicle liability insurance. In a few countries, there are funds covering more than two branches combined. Examples of classes other than motor vehicle liability are hunting (or shooting), workers' compensation, etc. These funds are closely related to the relevant **compulsory insurance** and supplement its functions. Almost all OECD countries require a car driver or owner to purchase liability insurance in order to protect victims of motor vehicle accidents by ensuring minimum indemnification for any damage or loss of income. As a rule, funds for compulsory motor vehicle liability insurance step in 1) when the driver responsible cannot be identified or is uninsured and thus unable to pay proper damages to the victim, or 2) when the insurer of the driver responsible is unable to pay the claim due to its financial difficulty or bankruptcy. In this sense, it should be stressed that this type of fund is mainly for the protection of accident victims, regardless of whether any insurance policy is involved or not. Nevertheless, they do provide a negligent driver with financial relief in the event that his insurer is unable to pay the claim. Concerning payment of claims, normally no limitation is imposed, or 100 per cent of a claim is paid, in view of the nature and purpose of the business involved, *i.e.* to protect victims of accidents. Reductions of, or caps on, payments could lead to insufficient compensation of the injured party or his family in the event of death.

2. ***General funds***: *i.e.*, funds covering either all **life insurance**, **non-life insurance** or both. At this writing, seven countries (Canada, Ireland, Japan, Korea, Poland, the United Kingdom and the United States) have adopted this type of fund. Unlike a fund for a specific class of insurance, general funds are triggered only when an insurer cannot meet claims by policyholders due to financial difficulty or insolvency. Normally, general funds exclude such classes as marine, transportation, aviation, **reinsurance**, etc., wherein the policyholders (ceding insurance companies in the case of reinsurance) involved can be considered to be professional, financially strong, and capable of making proper judgements as to which insurers to use and how to spread risks. It may also be important to note that, for similar reasons, enterprises

or individual policyholders with substantial net worth may not obtain compensation from a general fund. This exclusion is not normally applied in respect of compulsory insurance, which is also covered under the fund. General funds normally set certain limits, either by amount or by percentage, on their payments of claims, with the exception of compulsory lines of business. This is mainly because operation of a fund entails costs, which should be borne equitably by claimants who benefit from the fund. Another factor may be to give consumers an incentive to choose their insurers carefully and not merely succumb to the lure of cheaper rates. There seems to be a growing tendency to consider future introduction of general funds as a result of the recent instances of insolvency and financial difficulties affecting insurers in a number of OECD countries.

It is considered that **policyholder protection funds** should be relied upon as a last resort, after every possible measure has been made by the ailing insurer and/or the government to return the company to a sound commercial and financial footing. A couple of OECD countries have plans to create an "***early intervention arrangement***", which is a scheme to prevent an ailing insurer from becoming insolvent. This kind of scheme involves various arrangements ranging from reinsurance and/or transfer of the insurer's portfolio, to solvency support, *i.e.* injections of cash. It may therefore be regarded as another form of policyholder protection fund in the sense that it will be funded by participating insurers with the ultimate goal of protecting policyholders.

PREMIUMS

[*See also "Insurance Regulation and Supervision in Economies in Transition (1997)".*]

A **premium** can be defined as the selling price of insurance, *i.e.* the compensation paid by the insured party to the insurer in exchange for having the risk covered.

It is made up of the following components:

1. the ***pure premium*** (also called the ***net premium***), which corresponds to the average cost of a claim, multiplied by the

probability that the event being covered will occur. It also takes account of the duration of cover, the amount insured and interest rates, since there is a time-lag between the collection of the premium, which is generally paid in advance, and its use.

2. the ***loading***, which is added to the pure premium and can be broken down as follows:

- policy acquisition costs;
- premium collection costs;
- claims handling costs;
- administrative and general **expenses**;
- return on capital in non-mutual companies.

The sum of the pure premium and the loading for claims handling costs constitutes the ***risk premium***, which will be spent *pro rata* throughout the period of cover. The part of this risk premium spent at the close of a financial year is referred to as the ***earned risk premium***, while the remaining portion is called the ***unearned risk premium***. Depending on the legislation, some administrative expenses may be allocated to this risk premium.

Loading other than for claims handling costs is generally considered to be part of the writing cost, *i.e.* it is deemed to be fully spent or earned as soon as the policy is written or paid.

The sum of the pure premium and the loading constitutes the ***office premium***. Once any premium taxes are added, the ***total premium*** is obtained. In some countries, premium taxes typically are defined to be a part of the loading.

In life policies that guarantee the payment of capital, the price component representing the investment portion is known as the ***saving premium*** .

From a legal standpoint, depending on national legislation, premiums must be paid either at the policyholder's domicile, when collected by the insurer or its representative, or at the office of the insurer, when it is tendered by the policyholder.

As for the timing of payments, premiums may be paid either in advance (incl. *periodic premiums*, see below) or at the "end" of the policy term. In the latter case, a ***provisional premium*** is paid at the beginning of cover. Once the ***final or definite premium*** is calculated, based on data, such as earnings, turnover, or inventory, received from the policyholder at the end of the policy period, any difference shall be paid in or, in the event of overpayment, refunded. Normally a minimum premium is agreed. This kind of premium is also called ***audit premium*** .

A further timing distinction is made between ***periodic premiums***, payable at each due date specified in the policy, and ***single*** (or ***lump-sum***) ***premiums***. Periodic premiums are paid in ***instalment premiums***, these instalments being either monthly, quarterly, or half-yearly as opposed to ***annual premiums***.

As for a life company's portfolio management, premiums representing new business are known as ***cash premiums*** and premiums in respect of policy renewals are called ***renewal premiums***. Premiums added when a policy is modified by endorsement before the due date are called ***additional premiums***.

From an accounting standpoint, a premium is ***written*** when it is entered into the accounts at the time of billing by either the **insurance company** or by an agency or other authorised entity. However, in some countries premiums are entered into the accounts only after they are collected. If a customer refuses to pay a premium, it will be entered as a ***cancelled premium***, after having been recorded during a waiting period as a ***returned premium***. At the end of a period, any premium that is written and unpaid is overdue.

PROVISION FOR THE AGEING OF RISKS

This **technical provision** in health and invalidity insurance is also referred to as the **ageing provision** or **ageing reserve**. It is set aside to offset the increasing risk to insurers that arises as policyholders get older, whereas the **premiums** charged for long-term policies are flat by age category. Like technical **life insurance provisions**, the ageing reserve is calculated on an actuarial basis using morbidity and invalidity tables and is set aside in the initial years for each age category.

Depending on the applicable legislation, it is deemed to be either a reserve, *i.e.* a part of the surplus, or a technical provision, as in Denmark, Germany, and the Netherlands. In France, although a technical provision, it is not considered a tax-deductible expenditure.

PROVISION FOR UNEARNED PREMIUMS

[***See also, "Insurance Regulation and Supervision in Economies in Transition (1997)".***]

This provision is used to defer to the next period or to subsequent periods the proportions of gross **premiums** and risk premiums that are unearned at the close of the financial year.

The percentage of premiums to be carried forward can be computed:

- ***pro rata*** for each premium by dividing the number of days of coverage after the close of the financial year by the number of days of coverage granted by the receipt;

- by combining premiums having the same term (*e.g.* 12, 6 or 3 months, 1 month or any other term), each group being divided by the month in which premiums were written and each premium deemed to have been written in the middle of the month. Accordingly, any 12-month premium written in January will be considered to have been written on 15 January and will therefore provide coverage for 15 days beyond the closing date, *i.e.* 1/24th of the premium in question. A premium written in December of the same year will be deemed to take effect as of 15 December and provide coverage beyond the closing date of 23/24ths of the said premium (called ***twenty-fourths method***).

- Premiums can also be combined on a quarterly, rather than monthly, basis, in which case one refers to the ***eighths method*** .

- by applying a flat percentage to all premiums written during the financial year (called ***flat-rate method***).

Article 57 of Directive 91/674/EEC lays down the principle of separate computations for each contract but allows "the use of statistical methods, and in particular proportional and flat-rate methods, where they may be expected to give approximately the same results as individual calculations. In classes of insurance where the assumption of a temporal correlation between risk experience and premium is not appropriate, calculation methods shall be applied that take account of the differing pattern of risk over time."

It is clear that premiums written in arrears or in adjustment of prior years are not included, and that cancellations are deducted. Depending on local legislation and practice, such provisions may be used to defer portions of either gross premiums or risk premiums, *i.e.* gross premiums less deferred acquisition costs.

There are three possible accounting options:

- The provision may be shown as a liability, with deferred expenses implicitly deducted.
- The provision may be shown gross as a liability, and deferred **expenses** as an asset.
- The provision may be shown gross, and deferred expenses not booked as assets.

In **life insurance**, this provision may be subsumed under the **technical provision**. (see **LIFE INSURANCE PROVISIONS, OTHER NON-LIFE PROVISIONS, PROVISION FOR UNEXPIRED RISKS** and **EARNED PREMIUMS**)

PROVISION FOR UNEXPIRED RISKS

[*See also "Insurance Regulation and Supervision in Economies in Transition (1997)".*]

Over the years, and depending on the country, the term has encompassed concepts of variable scope.

In current EEC parlance, it refers to a provision that supplements the **provision for unearned premiums** if accounting or statistical data suggest that the latter may be inadequate to covers risks and **risk management** expenses after the end of the financial year.

Article 26 of Directive 91/674/EEC defines it thus: "the amount set aside in addition to unearned premiums in respect of risks to be borne by the insurance undertaking after the end of the financial year, in order to provide for all claims and **expenses** in connection with insurance contracts in force in excess of the related unearned premiums and any **premiums** receivable on those contracts."

As defined above, the provision is constituted if:

1. the provision for unearned premiums was computed using a flat-rate combining method but the average expiry dates within the groupings are significantly later than the median dates: *e.g.* if, in each month of the fourth quarter, a majority of three-month premiums were written in the last week of the month;

2. overall, loss experience and risk management expenses exceed the rate used to set premiums;

3. loss experience is not constant, and in particular, if losses occur more frequently in the early months of the year than in later months;

4. a rate increase has taken effect during the year, and its full impact will not be felt until the higher rates have been applied to each policy in the portfolio involved.

In common usage, and depending on the country and the era, the term has been used to refer to a broader concept -- that of the premiums that have to be allocated to the following year or to subsequent years in order to cover risks to be incurred on contracts in force at the valuation date.

This was the meaning in use in Latin countries before Community Directives were incorporated into their law, whereas the distinction between provisions for unearned premiums and provisions for unexpired risks already existed in the United Kingdom and Germany. In Belgium, provisions for unexpired risks include provisions for suspended risks, which cover partial refunds of premiums when vehicles are immobilised, whereas in France these estimated refunds are shown in a provision for premium refunds. In Luxembourg, there is a separate provision for such refunds, as there is in Germany.

The provision for unexpired risks as a supplement to the provision for unearned premiums -- or deferred premiums -- is calculated by extrapolating loss experience and risk-management expenses, *i.e.* the risk premium needed to cover the probable cost of losses to be incurred on contracts in force at the valuation date. Loss experience (LE) can be derived from the ratio, for the previous insurance period, of the burden of losses to **earned premiums** (EP), adjusted if necessary for seasonal variations. Risk management expenses are estimated from cost accounting figures, or a flat percentage is applied to premiums written.

Strictly, the provision for unearned premiums, net of deferred acquisition costs, plus the provision for unexpired risks has to be equal to:

Deferred gross premiums x [(LE/EP) + (Risk-management expenses/premiums written net of cancellations)].

Depending on the regulations, the provision covered by reinsurers can either be proportional to the gross provision or be defined by **treaties**. With regard to the balance sheet, the reinsurers' share is booked as an asset in Belgium, Denmark, France, Italy and Luxembourg, Portugal and Spain, while in Germany it is carried as a negative liability. In Ireland, the Netherlands and the United Kingdom, it is implicitly deducted from liabilities; in that case, the notes to financial accounts should disclose the details. In the United States, loss payments recoverable through **reinsurance** are shown as assets. (see **OTHER NON-LIFE PROVISIONS**)

PROVISIONS FOR OUTSTANDING CLAIMS

[*See also "Insurance Regulation and Supervision in Economies in Transition (1997)".*]

This **technical provision** corresponds to "the total estimated ultimate cost to an insurance undertaking of settling all claims arising from events which have occurred up to the end of the financial year, whether reported or not, less amounts already paid in respect of such claims" (Article 28, Directive 91/674/EEC). It is therefore composed of the following items:

- certain liabilities: the cost of claims settled administratively and/or legally, *i.e.* the final amount has been determined but payment has not yet been made;

- evaluated liabilities: the cost of claims reported but not yet settled because the adjustment of the claim has not yet been completed;

- estimated liabilities: the cost of ***claims incurred but not yet reported*** to the insurer (very often called ***IBNR***), including future claim-settlement **expenses**;

less

- recoveries from either third parties (***subrogation***) or the insured (***salvage***), if certain or highly probable;

- where applicable, a deduction to take account of a foreseeable delay in paying claims and thus of income from representative investments.

Theoretically, reported and unreported claims are assessed separately for each contract, the ***case basis method*** being the basic method of assessment. Depending on the regulations, a number of other methods may be used in conjunction with it, or in lieu thereof:

1. ***technical methods***: *a)* based on average costs in recent years, adjusted if necessary for inflation. This method can be applied to risks for which costs vary within a limited range, such as material automobile damage; *b)* based on accumulated payments over the previous three or five accounting periods, depending on the length of time it takes to settle claims. This method requires monetary stability, or at least low inflation, and continuity in the insurer's settlement policy.

2. a ***flat-rate method***: used on the understanding that rates are adequate for risks. Based on accounting data from an accounting period, a minimal provision is defined, equal to earned risk premiums less payouts in respect of the underwriting year. This method is sometimes referred to as the ***premium blocking*** or the ***period laundering method***. It is generally used in maritime insurance for the last two underwriting years.

IBNR is estimated on the basis of loss experience and, in particular, the claims pattern over several years. Recoveries and subrogation, as well as any salvage, are estimated on a prudent basis: some countries allow recoveries only if received within three months after the end of the financial year.

Future expenses for administering claim settlements are estimated, depending on national rules, using either a flat-rate method, *e.g.* one based on claims provisions, or analytical methods whereby the expenses allocated to the settlements function are estimated from accounting or statistical data.

Article 60 of Directive 91/674/EEC stipulates the rules applicable in the Community: "Statistical methods may be used if they result in an adequate provision having regard to the nature of the risks", although Member States may "make the application of such methods subject to prior approval."

Settlement expenses must be included irrespective of origin, whether internal or external.

Recovered losses may be deducted from the **provision for outstanding claims** or shown on the balance sheet as assets.

The discounting of outstanding claims is generally prohibited, since this practice could, in fact, prompt financially troubled companies to reduce their provisions in order to show a profit and could be allowed only if provisions were calculated on an actuarial basis, as they are in **life insurance**. Under the EU Directive, deductions are allowed if they are explicit, under very strict conditions. (see **OTHER NON-LIFE PROVISIONS**)

RATE REGULATION

Rate regulation strives to ensure that insurance rates are not *excessive, unfairly discriminatory* or *inadequate.* Inadequate competition within a market or lines of insurance can lead to excessive and sometimes inequitable rates. Supervisory officials also sometimes express concern that unrestrained price competition could lead to ruinous rate wars (with attendant inadequate rates) and massive insurer failures. Another rationale offered for rate **regulation** in some markets is the belief that citizens prefer a more orderly, less volatile market that strict rate regulation can provide.

It can be questioned whether rate regulation as a means of protecting against insolvencies is the most effective and efficient means of doing so. A possible exception is said to exist within a small market or with some economies in transition in which concern exists about predatory pricing; *i.e.*, where a large competitor charges insufficient premiums to drive competitors out of the market with the intention later to raise prices. Even here, a liberalised market should largely obviate the possibility of such predatorial pricing, assuming adequate **financial** and **competition regulation** exists.

A variety of rate regulation practices are found internationally. Governments or governmental sanctioned cartels set prices in some markets, especially in some developing countries. In other markets, governments set rate ceilings or rate increase limits. This occurs where policy makers contend that price competition is insufficient to avoid rate excessiveness.

Various forms of *ex ante* (prior approval) and *ex post* (subsequent disapproval) rate regulation exist, although most commercial lines of insurance internationally and nearly all **reinsurance** are free from rate regulation. With a ***prior approval*** system, insurers cannot use proposed rate schedules until they are officially approved by the regulator. A ***file-and-use*** system allows insurers to use a proposed rate schedule after filing it with the regulator. The regulator may later disapprove the rates, but failing this, the rates are deemed to be acceptable. Some countries have either no rating laws or permit open competition, although informational rate filings may be required. The EU Framework Directives have created a single insurance market in which *ex ante* rate regulation is largely abandoned, although joint loss data may be used and regulators retain broad rate oversight authority.

Internationally, it is common for different rules to apply to different classes of insurance, with those classes most closely connected to social policy (*e.g.*, compulsory automobile insurance) generally being subjected to greater rate oversight. Perhaps the line experiencing the most intensive rate regulation internationally is automobile liability (motor third-party) insurance.

Direct rate regulation in **life insurance** is the exception world-wide. Through mandated reserve requirements, however, life insurers in some markets often are subject to a type of indirect rate control. In other jurisdictions, the components of life insurance pricing (*e.g.*, mortality rates, interest rates, and **expenses**) may be subject to control, thus potentially precluding meaningful price competition.

RATING ORGANISATIONS

Rating organisations (or **agencies**) are independent firms that rate (grade) insurers based on the organisation's evaluation of the insurers' financial soundness and operations. Rating agencies typically use information provided by the insurer and publicly available financial and other information to derive their assessments. In general, these assessments take into consideration the insurer's asset depreciation and interest rate risks along with an evaluation of pricing adequacy within the general business environment. The most important factor is usually the insurer's capital position relative to these risks. The analysis will involve an examination of whether the insurer's capital is adequate to cover financial obligations under adverse economic and other circumstances.

Rating agencies use considerable discretion in the qualitative and quantitative factors that they use in rating insurers as well as in the methods employed. Particular insurer ratings represent the agency's opinion as to insurer soundness relative to other insurers in the industry. As such, ratings offer no guarantee of soundness, with the agencies having been criticised occasionally for their failure to anticipate some insurers' financial difficulties.

Rating agencies are, however, becoming more important in several countries. They may help to rectify partially the information asymmetry between insurance buyers -- who are often not well informed about insurers' financial condition -- and sellers who know their true financial condition but might have tenancies to minimise any adverse information. Many observers believe that ever greater competition will mean that rating agencies will become even more important in the future.

RECIPROCITY

The fair-trade concept of **reciprocity** can take on several meanings, each associated with a country responding to another country's actions. As a trade liberalisation and negotiation tool, reciprocity insists that trade concessions by one country should be matched in kind by its trading partners. Thus, if a country lowers its tariffs, reciprocity insists that its trading partners lower their tariffs in response. If the trading countries follow the **non-discrimination** principle, such reductions will apply to all trading partners.

At the international level, this type of reciprocity involves a process of ***offer and acceptance*** by which each negotiating country offers to eliminate or moderate certain existing trade restrictions. Each country either accepts the other countries' offers as sufficient in view of their own offers, or negotiates for better (meaning more liberal) offers. The objective is to have all countries' offers ultimately accepted, thus resulting in the successful conclusion of the trade round negotiations.

Another application of the reciprocity principle can, however, be trade restricting. So-called ***mirror-image reciprocity*** holds that trading partners will "mirror" the market access and other conditions followed by each other. An example will illustrate the concept. Assume that country A permits banks to sell insurance but country B does not. Under a **national treatment** standard and without reciprocity, banks from country B doing business in country A would be permitted by country A to sell insurance, and banks from country A doing business in country B would not be allowed by country B to sell insurance there.

Country A might contend that it provides better treatment to foreign banks than other countries (specifically country *B)* provide to its banks. Country A then adopts reciprocity rather than national treatment as its policy toward foreign firms. This means that country A would accord B's banks the same (mirror-image) market access and other treatment as country B extended to A's banks. Thus, country B's banks would be barred from selling insurance in country A because country B prohibits banks from selling insurance. Of course, country A's intent is to encourage country B to change (liberalise) its laws, but the practical effect can be to restrict rather than liberalise trade.

Reciprocity's goal (although not always its effect) is to encourage "good" behaviour by trading partners. **Retaliation**, a type of reciprocity is intended to punish or discourage "bad" behaviour.

REGIONAL TRADING ARRANGEMENTS

A **regional trading arrangement** is an agreement among governments to liberalise trade and possibly to co-ordinate other trade-related activities. There are four principal types of regional trading arrangements. ***A free trade area*** is a grouping of countries within which tariffs and non-tariff trade barriers between the members are generally abolished but with no common trade policy toward non-members. The North American Free Trade

Area (NAFTA) and the European Free Trade Association (EFTA) are examples of free trade areas.

A ***customs union*** is a free trade area that also establishes a common tariff and other trade policies with non-member countries. The Czech and Slovak Republics established a customs union to preserve previous commercial relationships between themselves and with third parties. The Arab Common Market is moving toward a customs union.

A ***common market*** is a customs union with provisions to liberalise movement of regional production factors (people and capital). The Southern Cone Common Market (MERCOSUR) of Argentina, Brazil, Paraguay and Uruguay is an example of a common market.

An ***economic union*** is a common market with provisions for the harmonisation of certain economic policies, particularly macroeconomic and regulatory. The EU is an example of an economic union.

Members of regional trading arrangements typically enjoy better **market access** to each other's markets than do non-members and sometimes other preferential trading concessions. Although technically inconsistent with the principle of **non-discrimination**, such arrangements are usually permitted under international trade agreements.

A concern by some observers is that regional trading arrangements could be perceived as a substitute for international trade agreements, so that support for world-wide trade liberalisation negotiations and agreements could wane. A further concern by some is that member countries of regional trading arrangements could conclude that liberalised trade among themselves was sufficient and, therefore, that trade barriers with respect to non-members could be more easily sustained. On the other hand, to the extent that regional trading arrangements can undertake a greater degree of liberalisation than can be negotiated under international auspices, they can promote freer trade internationally.

REGULATION

[*See also "OECD Insurance Guidelines" in the Annex.*]

(*Remark: the item is dealt with here very briefly and in an illustrative manner, as the issues it covers are treated in various other items. The reader is also invited to refer to the publication on "Insurance Regulation and Supervision in OECD Countries (1999.)*)

The most common rationale for **regulation** is to protect the public interest. Insurance regulation generally seeks to ensure that *quality, affordable* products are *available* from *reliable* insurers. Government intervention is usually most evident to ensure that insurers are *reliable*. In many, although a decreasing number, of developing countries, an additional goal may be the promotion of the domestic insurance industry and ensuring that the national insurance industry contributes to overall economic development.

If insurers are perceived as insecure, the system could easily break down. Many believe that private insurance cannot flourish without public confidence that it will function as promised and that government's duty is to ensure that this confidence is neither misplaced nor undermined.

Every country has insurance laws and regulations that determine who may sell and underwrite insurance and the circumstances under which they may do so. Minimum reserve, asset quality and quantity, and capital requirements are usually laid down. Special **accounting principles** are often mandated. **Rate regulation** is practised in several countries, along with regulation of policy conditions.

Regulation varies world-wide. Countries that follow the traditional continental European model of regulation have focused more on stability and market order. Countries that follow the Anglo-Saxon model have placed primary reliance on the market to set rates and allocate resources.

Government oversight of insurance markets typically takes place at three levels. *First*, parliament or other legislative body enacts laws to establish the country's broad legal framework for insurance and to prescribe the general standards and scope of responsibilities governing the activities of the administrative agency charged with enforcement of the insurance laws. These laws address the major components of insurance oversight which may include some or all of the following:

- formation and licensing of insurers for the various classes of insurance and **reinsurance**
- the licensing of agents and **brokers**
- the filing and approval of insurance rates
- the filing and approval of proposal material and policy forms
- unauthorised insurance and unfair trade practices
- insurer financial reporting, examination and other financial requirements
- rehabilitation and **liquidation** of insurers
- guaranty funds **(policyholder protection funds)**
- insurance product and company taxation (see **TAXATION OF INSURANCE PRODUCTS**)

Courts are the *second* mechanisms of government oversight. The judiciary has a threefold role in insurance oversight. It resolves disputes between insurers and policyholders. It enforces civil and sometimes criminal penalties against those who violate insurance laws. Finally, insurers and insurance intermediaries occasionally resort to the courts trying to overturn arbitrary or unconstitutional statutes and administrative regulation or orders promulgated by the insurance supervisor.

The *third* area of government oversight falls under the state's executive branch. Because of the many complexities in insurance, policy makers ordinarily delegate discretionary authority to administrative officials to supervise the insurance business. (see **SUPERVISION**) The department or agency charged by the legislature with enforcement of the nation's insurance laws will have broad administrative, quasi-legislative and quasi-judicial powers.

The EU regulatory situation is unique. One of the principal means of establishing minimum regulatory harmonisation among the 15 EU member countries is through directives. A ***directive*** is an order issued by the EU's Council of Ministers that requires member countries to enact new national laws or alter existing laws to come into compliance with the directive's provisions. Directives are meant to establish minimum harmonisation of essential regulation throughout the EU. They are the principal means by which the EU is creating its single market.

REINSURANCE

[*See also "OECD Insurance Guidelines" in the Annex and "Insurance Regulation and Supervision in Economies in Transition (1997).*]

Insurance purchased by insurers to hedge their own insurance portfolios is classed as **reinsurance**. Reinsurance is sold by ***professional reinsurers***, which deal in reinsurance only, and by some direct writing companies through their reinsurance departments.

Almost all insurers world-wide purchase reinsurance. Reinsurers themselves purchase reinsurance (*i.e.*, they ***retrocede*** business to other reinsurers.) Dozens of insurers and reinsurers world-wide would typically participate on insurance policies with high limits.

The amount of insurance an insurer keeps for itself is called the ***retention*** and the amount of the insurance ceded to the reinsurer is known as the ***cession***. In return for assuming risk, the reinsurer receives a reinsurance premium and agrees to indemnify the ceding company for claims falling within the terms of the reinsurance agreement. (see **REINSURANCE TREATIES**)

Reinsurance is used for several reasons. First, by limiting the primary company's liability, reinsurance allows insurers to write more business and for higher limits. Without reinsurance or some other mechanism for transferring liability, many companies would be restricted in the amount of coverage they could safely retain.

Reinsurance can help stabilise profits for direct writing companies. By limiting the maximum size of losses for which the direct writing company is responsible, great fluctuations in profits are minimised.

Reinsurance also provides considerable protection to the ceding company against catastrophic losses caused by natural disasters such as earthquakes and hurricanes and by human-made disasters such as oil pollution. Without reinsurance, the impact of such catastrophic losses might be greater than the primary company could absorb.

Reinsurance can offer a form of financing for primary companies. With certain types of reinsurance, the insurer receives a ***ceding commission*** from the reinsurer to cover acquisition **expenses**. This commission offsets some of the direct writing company's expenses, thus minimising the cash flow drain associated with writing new business.

Finally, reinsurers often provide advice and assistance to primary insurers on underwriting procedures and in claims handling. This assistance can be of particularly great value to a new insurer or to one that is entering a new line of business.

Research has confirmed that the likelihood of reinsurance usage increases: 1) the smaller the **insurance company**, 2) the larger the maximum possible claim under policies, and 3) the higher the covariance of policy payoffs with the existing set of company policies.

Reinsurance typically involves exposures with large and highly variable loss potential. As such, great underwriting and pricing expertise are required. Reinsurance tends to be highly specialised and is probably the most international insurance business.

The insured often is unaware that the insurer has reinsured the policy. This fact ordinarily poses no difficulties as the insured's legal relationship is with the direct writing company, not the reinsurer. The direct writing company remains obligated to pay legitimate claims under the reinsured policy, even if the reinsurer is unable to do so. Some reinsurer failures, however, have resulted in the failure of direct writing insurers.

As the direct writing company ordinarily is a knowledgeable buyer and the reinsurer is a knowledgeable seller, government intervention into the transaction has historically been non-existent or kept to a minimum. During the past few years, however, the issue of reinsurance security has been of great concern to many insurance regulators because of its importance to primary insurers' financial stability.

OECD adopted in March 1998 "The Recommendation of the Council on Assessment of Reinsurance Companies" to promote the assessment by insurance companies of their reinsurers' solvency. The Recommendation provides a list of technical criteria to help insurance companies in assessing reinsurers financial situation, especially in the absence or lack of reliable information in this respect.

REINSURANCE TREATIES

[*See also "Insurance Regulation and Supervision in Economies in Transition (1997)".*]

A **treaty** or a **reinsurance treaty** is a contract between a direct **insurance company** (called ***cedant***) and a reinsurer, whereby the reinsurer undertakes to assume (or reinsure)—and normally the cedant undertakes to cede—all risks falling into the categories agreed in advance between the two parties. Treaties can be divided into two types:

1. ***proportional treaties***, whereby both parties share the risk proportionally with regard to **premiums** and losses;

2. ***non-proportional treaties***, whereby the reinsurer agrees to pay some or all of the excess over an agreed amount in respect of a loss incurred by the cedant. Premiums are calculated independently.

One special type of treaty is the ***facultative-obligatory treaty***, whereby the cedant is under no obligation to cede risks, but the reinsurer must accept whatever risks the cedant chooses to cede. This is also called an ***open-cover***.

On the other hand, ***facultative reinsurance*** may be used for very large risks which treaties cannot absorb, and unique risks for which it is difficult to establish a reinsurance treaty. Under facultative reinsurance, a risk is individually offered by the cedant and accepted by reinsurers only when it meets their underwriting criteria.

When two companies exchange **reinsurance**, whether treaties or facultative business, to enhance the spreading of risks, the resultant transaction is called a ***reciprocal exchange***.

Proportional treaties can be further broken down into:

a) ***quota-share treaties***, whereby the insurer cedes a given percentage of the relevant premiums to the reinsurer, who in return accepts the same percentage of the corresponding claims;

b) ***surplus (line) treaties***, whereby the cedant, based on the prescribed ***table of limits*** , must retain a portion of the risk (this retention is called a ***line***) and may cede a given number of lines , a stipulated percentage of which the reinsurer is required to accept. Premiums and the corresponding losses are allocated proportionally between the cedant and the reinsurers. This type of treaty is also referred to as an ***excess of line treaty*** .

Non-proportional treaties are generally divided into:

a) ***excess of loss treaties***, whereby the cover applies only to the portion of a claim above a specific amount, known as the **priority** or **excess point** . The ceding insurer pays a lump-sum premium, occasionally with a premium adjustment clause, normally calculated on the basis of a ***burning cost***, which is a method of premium calculation taking into consideration the amount of recovery in the past (*e.g.* over the past five years) under the cover. This treaty is also called ***X/L*** for short.

   On the one hand, this kind of treaty can be used as a ***working cover*** or ***per risk cover*** , whereby the limit and excess point apply to individual claims, typically in automobile and fire insurance. In some cases, an annual aggregate limit is established to cap the reinsurer's liability. On the other hand, it can also be used as a ***catastrophe cover***, whereby the limit and excess point apply to aggregate claims under separate branches such as fire, automobile, and personal accidents, arising out of any one catastrophic event (*e.g.* earthquakes, hurricanes, floods, airplane crash etc.).

b) ***stop-loss treaties*** (or ***excess of loss ratio treaties***), whereby the limit and excess point are set in terms of a specified loss ratio (*i.e.* the amount of annual aggregate losses divided by the amount of annual premiums) for the business covered. It is not unusual to cap recovery from the reinsurers by the amount of losses. The purpose of this type of treaty is to spread the total loss experience due to cyclical risks such as hail, credit, natural disasters etc. over a period of at least five years. The ceding insurer pays a lump-sum premium calculated by a similar method as in excess of loss treaties.

RETALIATION

Retaliation occurs when a jurisdiction in some way restricts access to its market in response to a trading partner's restricting access or failure to lower existing trade barriers to its market. The threat of retaliation can lead to liberalisation. Thus, if one country believes another is engaging in practices that restrict trade unduly, it might threaten to retaliate if the offending country fails to loosen the restrictions. The threat of retaliation, especially if made by a major trading partner, can cause the country to undertake liberalising actions.

Retaliation, however, can be a risky trade weapon. If one country increases protection against imports, its trading partners may do similarly. The effect can result in trade wars of the type that contributed to the 1930s Great Depression.

RISK MANAGEMENT

Risk management is the set of procedures used to identify, evaluate and deal with risks. These procedures usually include the ***risk management process*** which involves 1) identification and evaluation of the possible outcomes associated with events or activities, 2) exploration of the techniques to deal constructively with these risks, and 3) implementation and periodic review of a logical plan of action. Most large businesses and governments have departments dedicated to risk management.

Risk management historically has been concerned mainly with situations whose outcomes involve losses, without the possibility of gain. As such, it was often closely identified with insurance, one of the means of financing losses. However, this view of risk management is changing as corporate executives and government officials realise that a fragmented approach to the management of risk is less effective and efficient than an integrated approach which involves all the risks to which an organisation is exposed. Such a holistic approach includes situations where a range of outcomes exists, from a gain to a loss.

Thus, risk management may be concerned with the efficient and effective management of any or all of the following types of risks:

- ***Business risk*** (related to market developments)

- ***Credit risk*** (*e.g.*, chance of creditor default)

- ***Exchange rate risk*** (*e.g.*, loss or gain from transactions in different currencies)

- ***Hazard risk*** (*e.g.*, loss from fire, windstorm, etc.)

- ***Inflation risk*** (*e.g.*, loss or gain in assets or income from inflation)

- ***Interest rate risk*** (*e.g.*, loss or gain in value from a fixed-rate bond)

- ***Liquidity risk*** (*e.g.*, chance of illiquidity because of non-marketability of assets)

- ***Political risk*** (*e.g.*, nationalisation)

Many of these risks are dealt with effectively through organisational monitoring. Some (*e.g.*, exchange rate risk and inflation risk) might be amenable to hedging in the capital market. Others can be financed through commercial insurance or export/import insurance normally operated by the government (*e.g.*, hazard risk and political risk). Many large corporations use captive insurers and other self-funding techniques. (see **RISKS FACED BY INSURANCE COMPANIES**)

RISKS FACED BY INSURANCE COMPANIES

The risks **insurance companies** face can be broken down into four broad categories:

- underwriting risks;

- reinsurance risks;

- investment risks;

- exogenous risks.

1. The two greatest ***underwriting risks*** are "inadequate rating" and the risk of "underestimating future commitments", each of which can have an impact on the other. If they are to charge adequate **premiums**, insurers must, based on their own experience or

industry or national statistics, determine their technical costs, calculate the loading for administrative **expenses** and estimate the financial returns generated through the inversion of the production cycle. The resulting market price should be in a range that is competitive, but that complies with regulatory requirements.

The main causes of inadequate rating are as follows:

- unreliable statistics;
- a discrepancy between estimates and outcomes because the portfolio is too small, major losses incurred are disproportionate to the size of the portfolio and the amount of **reinsurance**, or there is an unexpected variation in the frequency of claims;
- unfavourable discrepancies in mortality or morbidity rates because of the use of outdated tables.

Underestimates of commitments are generally due to the following:

- the use of historical rates that are too low, to calculate the following provisions:
  - **provisions for unearned premiums**: the deferred premiums are insufficient to cover claims;
  - **mathematical provisions**: the same results as above;
  - provisions for claims incurred but not reported: the commitments are based on inadequate risk premiums.
- miscalculation of policy costs by underwriters, including loading for administrative expenses;
- a voluntary reduction of commitments: losses are carried forward to following years in order to enhance the current year's accounts;

These causes can be made worse by an unbalanced portfolio in which long-term classes or classes being liquidated predominate, while management expenses continue to rise.

2. The ***reinsurance risks*** that companies face are as follows:

   - difficulties in finding reinsurance because of: chronic gross technical deficits that reinsurers cannot cover at a cost that the ceding insurer can afford;
   - the low premium basis of the risks being ceded, which rules out spreading losses over a number of years;
   - the possibility that the reinsurer will gain control of the ceding insurer because of the large proportion of business ceded;
   - insolvency of the reinsurer because of insufficient deposits or collateral.

3. ***Investment, credit or financial risks*** stem from the large size of the assets managed by the insurer on behalf of policyholders or beneficiaries, which are subject to requirements as to profitability, safety, availability and matching and must be equivalent to the insurer's technical commitments.

   - The main risks are as follows:
     - the ***risk of a slump*** in a market or a part of a market, such as the recent property crisis in the United Kingdom, which reduced insurers' cover of their commitments;
     - ***interest rate risk***: faced with stiff competition, insurance companies offer increasingly attractive products, although they may not be able in the future to find assets with yields sufficient to cover the corresponding liabilities;
     - ***credit risk***: cover in the form of loans and other receivables can depreciate because of the borrower's insolvency;
     - ***risks linked to strategic choices***: a policy of expansion through outside growth can lead a company to buy shares that are overvalued in relation to their growth potential;
     - ***liquidity risk***: if a major loss occurs or policies are surrendered on a massive scale because increasingly attractive products are being marketed, an insurer may have to realise assets on unfavourable terms;

- ***risks related to off-balance sheet liabilities***, *i.e.* endorsements, suretyship or guarantees given to third parties, especially commitments made to subsidiaries;
- ***risks specific to conglomerates***: when a group includes an insurer, a reinsurer and/or a bank, there is a danger that credit will be transferred or that equity capital will be used twice over within the conglomerate; a captive reinsurer can be used by the insurer to ease its solvency margin requirement, while the bank's net assets can be used both to meet the insurer's solvency margin and its own Cooke ratio (see **FINANCIAL SERVICES CONGLOMERATES**);
- the ***exchange rate risk***: If an insurer holds investments in currencies other than those in which the liabilities are likely to be paid in the future, there is the possibility that the currency in which the investments are held might have depreciated by the time claims have to be paid.

4. ***Exogenous risks*** refer to the following aspects of a company's environment:

   - economic and financial environment: risks linked to a change in the inflation path, *i.e.* a given trend has been used to forecast future needs for **technical provisions** and the solvency margin; the risk of a take-over or merger; risks linked to a crisis in other sectors; an increase in the number of fraudulent claims;
   - technological environment: technological changes and the company's ability to respond rapidly to them;
   - legal environment: the trend towards higher awards by courts, especially in motor vehicle liability cases. (see **RISK MANAGEMENT**).

SOLVENCY RULES

[*See also "OECD Insurance Guidelines" in the Annex, "Policy Issues in Insurance (1996)" and "Insurance Solvency Supervision (1995)".*]

(Remark: the item is dealt with here very briefly and in an illustrative manner, as the issues it covers are treated in various other items. The reader is also invited to refer to the publication on "Insurance Regulation and Supervision in OECD Countries (1999.)

There are two aspects to insurer solvency:

- the adequacy of **technical provisions**, as assessed through the ***solvency margin***;
- the capacity to cover all other, non-technical, risks, as assessed in terms of ***risk-based capital (RBC)***.

A company's solvency margin, under EU rules, is roughly equal to its assets net of liabilities, *i.e.* to the total of paid-up capital and reserves after the allocation of profit. To this accounting value of the enterprise a number of adjustments are made, including the amount by which the estimated market value of investments on the last day of the year exceeds book value. This margin must not be less than the statutory requirement:

1. **non-life insurance:** There are two possible methods. The one yielding the greater amount is adopted:

   - Based on gross written **premiums**, for direct and assumed business: After application of a "coefficient taking into account the relief brought by ceded **reinsurance**", the required margin is 18 per cent for the first ECU 7 million and 16 per cent thereafter.

   - Based on average gross claims incurred over the past three years: After the same ceded reinsurance coefficient is applied, the required margin is 26 per cent for the first ECU 10 million and 23 per cent thereafter.

2. **life insurance**: The method generally adopted is to require 4 per cent on **mathematical provisions** and 0.3 per cent on capital at risk.

The relief coefficient for ceded reinsurance is the ratio of net loss incurred to gross loss incurred during the financial year; this coefficient cannot be less than 0.50 in non-life or less than 0.85 in life.

The concept of risk-based capital, which was first introduced in United States in 1992, assesses risks in terms of the quality of a company's assets and liabilities. It is inspired by the ***Cooke ratio***, which is applicable to banks: each category of asset is assigned a risk factor whose weighting increases with the degree of inherent risk.

For life and health insurance, the applicable risk categories are: risk with respect to assets, risk of adverse insurance experience with respect to liabilities and obligations, interest rate risk and all other business risks.

In property and casualty insurance, a distinction is made between the following risks:

- R1: investments in securities and real estate.

- R2: investments in subsidiaries and other affiliates.

For these two categories, the regulatory authorities weight the risk factors, which vary with the volatility of an investment's market value as well as with its marketability. In addition, the ten largest investments have double weighting. Conversely, an adjustment is made to allow for the degree of diversification of the investment portfolio.

- R3: receivables, consisting primarily of recoverable reinsurance; All such receivables have a risk factor of 10 per cent, with no distinction for a company's quality or nationality. Examples of other items included in this category are interest and dividends receivable.

- R4: provisions for loss and loss adjustment **expenses**, taking the following elements into account:
  - the extent to which provisions might be exceeded in a worst-case scenario;
  - the provision's worst development year for the past ten years;
  - the possibility of upward or downward adjustment for concentration or diversification of risks, a multi-line insurer having a lower risk factor than a single-line company;

    - growth in written premiums, with a risk factor applying if average annual growth has exceeded 10 per cent over the preceding three years.

- R5: written premium risk, reflecting the possibility that premiums written during the following year may be insufficient to pay future claims, the insurer's diversification or concentration, and whether or not average annual growth has exceeded 10 per cent over the preceding three years;

- R0: off balance sheet risk: examples of risks not appearing on the balance sheet include parent-company guarantees to meet the commitments of subsidiaries.

To calculate risk-based capital, it will be necessary to aggregate the above items, but an adjustment is made to take account of the fact that it is virtually impossible that all of these risks would actually occur simultaneously. They might even compensate each other. The effect of the adjustment is to reduce the amount of required capital by approximately 40 per cent.

Risk-based capital will be given by the following formula:

$$C = \sqrt{(R0) + (R1)^2 + (R2)^2 + (R3)^2 + (R4)^2 + (R5)^2}$$

This does not really constitute a minimum solvency margin, since regulators intervene before capital is reduced to this level. [see **FINANCIAL (PRUDENTIAL) REGULATION** and **RISKS FACED BY INSURANCE COMPANIES**]

SPREAD AND DIVERSIFICATION OF INVESTMENTS

[*See also "OECD Insurance Guidelines" in the Annex and "Policy Issues in Insurance (1996)".*]

The investments that cover an insurer's technical commitments towards policyholders and beneficiaries are subject to certain rules regarding safety, rate of return and liquidity. One of these is the rule that investments must be spread and diversified between various assets.

Firstly, it is common to find within the insurance legislation lists of approved classes of financial assets that can be held. These approved investments (called ***admissible investments***) are those which are considered to have acceptable levels of default and liquidity risk. Some countries have more restrictive lists of approved investments than others. There has been a general trend in recent years in most OECD countries for regulations to be liberalised, with more classes of financial assets to be permitted.

Secondly, there are maximum percentages of total investments that can be held in a given class of investment. These maximum limits are on the classes of investment which are deemed to have higher levels of default or liquidity risk. Hence, it is common to find maxima on unquoted securities, on low quality corporate bonds and on certain classes of foreign investments. In a few countries, there are minima on classes of investment possessing low risk, usually government securities or high quality bonds; however, there has been a general move away in recent years from these minima. Currently, no OECD countries adopt this minimum limit. EU Member States are, in fact, not permitted to require insurers to invest in particular categories of assets. Maximum percentages on classes of investment have a double purpose in risk reduction: (a) they seek to restrict holdings in classes of investment which are deemed to be risky; and (b) they are set to ensure adequate diversification of the investment portfolio as a whole.

Thirdly, there are **investment regulations** which place a maximum limit on the proportion of total investments that can be held in a single investment. These maxima usually apply to investments in the securities of one company or in one piece of real estate. The purpose of these maxima are again to ensure adequate portfolio diversification.

For example, in the EU, the Member State of origin has to set a maximum percentage for investments in relation to total gross **technical provisions**, which have to correspond, at the highest, to the following figures:

– any one piece of land or building, or a number of pieces of land and buildings close enough to each other to be considered as being effectively one investment: 10 per cent;

– money market or financial instruments from the same undertaking, and loans granted to a single borrower other than those to a State, regional or local authority or an international organisation to which at least one Member State belongs: 5 per cent (this limit may be raised to 10 per cent if an undertaking does not invest more than 40 per cent of its gross technical provisions in the loans or securities of issuing bodies and borrowers in each of which it has invested more than 5 per cent of its assets);

- unsecured loans other than those granted to credit institutions and **insurance companies**, and to investment companies established in a Member State, up to a limit of 1 per cent for any one unsecured loan: 5 per cent;
- cash in hand: 3 per cent;
- shares, similar securities and bonds not traded on a regulated market: 10 per cent.

These provisions may be waived at the insurer's request in exceptional circumstances for a temporary period or under a properly reasoned decision.

SUPERVISION

[*See also "OECD Insurance Guidelines" in the Annex.*]

(Remark: the item is dealt with here very briefly and generally, as the issues it covers are treated in various other items. The reader is also invited to refer to the publication on "Insurance Regulation and Supervision in OECD Countries (1999)". The text below is thus illustrative only.)

Insurance **supervision** is part of the executive power and it usually comes within the competence of the finance or economics minister, or the minister of justice in one country. In majority of the countries, supervision is carried out by a special institution called the insurance supervisory authority. It may be either a special department in the competent ministry or a separate subordinate authority of the ministry or even both. The responsibility of the supervisory authority differs in the individual countries. Generally, the supervisory authority carries out on-going supervision of the **insurance companies** while certain basic decisions are frequently left to the minister. (See **REGULATION**)

In all Member countries, the insurance companies carrying on direct insurance are subject to supervision. It extends to, as a rule, to all classes of insurance. If apart from direct insurance the insurance companies also carry on **reinsurance**, the latter will also be supervised. Companies specialised in reinsurance, so called ***professional reinsurance companies,*** are equally supervised in several Member countries. Some Member countries only control the accounts of such companies and others do not control them at all. Foreign insurance companies are subject to supervision in all Member countries if they operate in the country through a branch which carries on direct insurance business. (See **CROSS-BORDER INSURANCE TRADE**)

Individuals or companies acting as intermediaries for insurance policies are also subject to supervision in a growing number of countries.

As highlighted in the OECD Insurance Guidelines (see Annex), the duties of supervisory authorities generally focus on the following areas:

- supervision with respect to legal obligations: compliance with existing legal provisions, by-laws of the company, general terms and conditions of insurance policies;
- financial supervisions: own funds, **technical provisions**, assets, monitoring of business activities;
- audit of interim and annual financial statements;
- actuarial supervision: tariffs, technical or **mathematical provisions**;
- management supervision: fit and proper requirements of company officers, reputation of strategic shareholders;
- economic supervision ; conditions prevailing in the marketplace, statistics.

The supervisory function generally proceeds through three main axes: licensing (before insurance operations), supervision of insurance operations and treatment of difficulties: recovery measures and/or suspension and termination of the operations.

1. Licensing: Insurance companies which wish to take up direct insurance business must obtain a special licence in all Member countries. Reinsurance companies must obtain a licence only in some Member countries. The licence is granted by way of an

administrative act. In some Member countries it comes within the competence of the relevant minister and in others of the supervisory authority. In all Member countries an insurance company has to meet certain requirements before it is granted a licence. These are legal, financial, accounting, and technical requirements. Most Member countries and all EU Member states demand that the bases of operations be included by the insurance companies in a **business plan**, which has to be submitted to the competent authority which grants the licence. Insurance companies wishing to obtain a licence for a branch or agency in a country other than the country where they have their head office also have to meet similar requirements. (see **AUTHORISATION**)

2. Supervision of operations: In all Member countries, the insurance companies are subject to on-going supervision after they have been authorised to take up business. The conditions under which the licence has been granted must also be observed in future. They also have to be adapted to future business developments. The activity of insurance supervision may be quite comprehensive. It is manifold and its control extends to the legal, financial, accounting, technical, and economic aspects of insurance operations. In some Member countries the supervisory authority supervises the overall operations of an insurance company and thus exercises control mainly to financial and accounting aspects. Insurance supervision is carried out in two different ways in all Member countries:

- The supervisory authority supervises the business activities of the insurance company on the basis of the documents to be submitted and other documents available to it (***on-going supervision***). On-going supervision involves legal control, financial control on capital requirement (solvency), technical provisions, investments, control of accounts, technical control (tariffs), and economic control [see **FINANCIAL (PRUDENTIAL) SUPERVISION**];

- The supervisory authority, in addition to on-going supervision, may inspect the operations of the insurance company at its offices and checks all the documents which are thought to be of importance (***on-site inspection***). This enables the supervisory authority to make sure that the documents submitted reflect the actual situation, on the one hand, and to obtain additional information about the business practices of the insurance company, on the other hand. Object and scope of the inspection, selection of the inspectors as well as motive and frequency of the inspections vary across individual countries.

3. Treatment of the difficulties: the supervisory body will take recovery measures (see ***recovery plan***) or will even possibly request the suspension or termination of the operations. (see **SUSPENSION AND TERMINATION**)

SUSPENSION AND TERMINATION

[***See also "Policy Issues in Insurance (1996)" and "Insurance Solvency Supervision (1995)"***.]

Suspension or termination of business operations may affect all or only part of the classes of insurance for which the **insurance company** was granted licence. The suspension or termination of business operations may be voluntary, *i.e.* by a decision taken by the insurance company, or compulsory by order of the supervisory authority.

- ***Voluntary suspension***: In most OECD Member countries, the insurance companies may suspend business in one or several classes of insurance without giving any reasons for this. Most countries require that the insurance company inform the supervisory authority about the suspension. The suspension does not necessarily result in the withdrawal of the licence to do business in the relevant class. In many Member countries, however, there are provisions stipulating the maximum period of time of such a suspension. If the relevant class is not resumed within the period, the licence expires or is withdrawn.

- ***Voluntary termination***: In most Member countries, the insurance companies may terminate business operations in all or certain classes of insurance for different reasons. The supervisory authority has to be informed accordingly. In most Member countries, termination of business operations results in the expiry or withdrawal of the licence for the relevant class of insurance or total insurance business. The existing insurance policies have to be wound up or transferred to another insurer.

- *Compulsory suspension*: Not in all Member countries is the supervisory authority entitled to order a compulsory suspension of the business operations of an insurer in individual classes of insurance or of its entire insurance business. Where there is such a possibility, this measure serves, as a rule, to make the insure remedy any abuses and to prevent any negative effects for the insured. If the insurer meets its obligations, the suspension order is cancelled. Otherwise, the next step, as a rule, would be to withdraw the licence and thus to terminate business operations.

- *Compulsory termination*: In most Member countries, the licence to do insurance business may, under certain conditions, be withdrawn for the entire business or a certain class of insurance. The insurance company then has to terminate business operations. Accordingly, it is no longer permitted to write new business or to extend or renew any existing contracts. After compulsory termination of all business operations, the existing portfolio has to be wound up. It may, however, also be transferred to another insurer. If only the licence for a particular class of insurance is withdrawn, the insurer continues its other activities. Only in the class for which the licence has been withdrawn are the insurance contracts wound up or transferred to another company.

- **Liquidation**: Liquidation means the winding up of the entire company business. It is carried out if the insurance company definitely discontinues its business operations. It may be carried out on a voluntary or compulsory basis. Liquidation is terminated when the insurance company has met all claims. In most Member countries, it is terminated earlier if the existing means are not sufficient to satisfy all creditors' claims. In this case the insurer is insolvent and thus requires to be wound up. (see also special item on this issue.)

TAXATION OF INSURANCE PRODUCTS

[*See also "Policy Issues in Insurance (1996)".*]

The main purpose of taxation is, in general, to raise revenue for the state, but it also facilitates the attainment of economic and social goals. Under this item, taxation of **life insurance** products is discussed for illustration and in view of their nature as very important financial instruments.

1. Life insurance products taxation

The extent and nature of tax concessions vary from being relatively minor and designed to simplify tax administration to being substantial and designed to encourage life insurance purchase or maintenance. This exploration of the tax treatment of life products is structured around life product cash flow components: **premiums**, living benefits and death benefits.

- Premiums

Several OECD countries provide tax relief on premiums paid for qualifying life insurance policies under the income taxation. Such tax concession is intended to encourage the purchase of life insurance. In general, where granted, tax concessions apply to policies whose exclusive or predominant purpose is to provide living benefits, such as endowments and annuities. Concessions are less commonly extended to policies whose purposes are exclusively or predominantly to provide death benefits. Also, tax concessions are frequently denied when consumers purchase otherwise qualifying policies from unlicensed or foreign insurers. As regards the tax treatment of premiums paid by employers on employee life insurance products, the general rule in the OECD countries seem to be that employer contributions for qualified employee benefit plans are tax deductibles by the employer and often not taxable to the employee, although this treatment varies by country.

- Living benefits

In most OECD countries, payments by life insurers for so-called living benefits exceed payouts resulting from insured deaths. Living benefit payouts or accruals may be classified broadly into three categories.

The first category comprises dividends (bonuses) under participating (with benefits) contracts. The general rule in OECD countries is that dividends paid do not cause current taxable income. Countries follow this practice because of the complexity entailed in any attempt to identify the excess investment income component within dividends.

The second category relates to policy cash values and maturity (capital sum) amounts. OECD countries generally do not directly tax interest credited on policy cash values - the so-called ***inside interest build up***. One reason for this favourable treatment relates again to the complexity in trying to do otherwise.

The third category constitutes payouts under annuity contracts. The inside interest build up of annuities during their accumulation period usually receives the same tax treatment as other life insurance products. In most OECD countries, various mechanisms are prescribed in which the excess of payments received over premiums paid is taxed, usually on some type of prorata basis over the annuity payout period.

- Death proceeds

Most OECD countries exempt death proceeds paid under qualifying life insurance policies from income taxation. A cash value policy's death proceeds can be viewed as comprised partly of the cash value. As noted above, the interest component of the cash value typically would not have been taxed during the insured's lifetime. As it is not taxed on death, it thereby can escape income taxation altogether. Governments commonly levy estate duties (taxes), measured on the value of property that a decedent owed, controlled or transferred. Life insurance death proceeds are subject to estate duties in most OECD countries. In most of these instances, however, provision is made for special circumstances that can lead to the proceeds being excluded, in whole or in part, from assessment.

2. Life insurance company taxation

The tax treatment at the corporate (supplier) level should not be ignored as it can affect product value. Life insurer taxation typically is of two types: premium taxation and net income taxation.

- ***Premium taxation***

Several OECD countries levy taxes on insurers' premium revenues. Premium taxes are the most common, but some countries levy stamp duties and other assessments. The insurer is responsible for tax payment in the great majority of countries, although the insured may be responsible when business is placed with an unlicensed insurer. Even with the insurer responsible for payment, such taxation is closely related to policyholder taxation. Under the typical premium tax structure, the tax base is the simple total of the insurer's premium revenue (excluding assumed reinsurance premiums), with certain alterations. Most jurisdictions permit a deduction from the tax base for dividends paid to policyholders. Most countries do not levy premium taxes on annuity considerations paid to insurers. Even those states that tax annuity considerations typically exempt contributions to qualified retirement annuity plans or tax them at a lower rate.

- ***Income taxation***

Life insurers typically are taxed on some variation of net income in OECD countries, in much the same way as other companies are taxed. Determining life insurance profit is a challenge. The challenge arises from the difference in timing between premium payments and claim payments. The typical tax base for purposes of calculating taxable income is the sum of investment and premium income. The yearly increase in policy reserves, acquisition and administrative expenses, policy dividends paid, and premiums paid on ceded reinsurance may be deducted from this sum. Other deductions may be permitted and special rules may exist for loss carryovers and (domestic and foreign) branch income.

TECHNICAL PROVISIONS (RESERVES)

[*See also "Insurance Regulation and Supervision in Economies in Transition (1997)" and "Insurance Solvency Supervision (1995)".*]

According to EU terminology, **technical provisions** refer to an insurer's liabilities under the contracts it has written.

Under EU directives, a liability may also be booked as either a technical provision or a contingency reserve: for example, if the term ***equalisation*** is understood to mean a legal or an administrative requirement to smooth out the claims ratio resulting from variations in the loss experience of individual years, it will be a provision, as in Denmark, France, Germany, Italy, the Netherlands, and Spain. In Belgium and Luxembourg, where a correction may be set up at a company's discretion, the term should be reserve, while the intention is to equalise and stabilise results over time. As for credit insurance, the Third Directive refers to an **equalisation reserve** calculated by four methods which will not yield similar values for the reserve and for the equalisation of fluctuations.

Another example of the fine lines of distinction between provisions and reserves in respect of specific items of liability is the valuation adjustment for redeemable securities covering technical provisions in France: French legislation allows a capitalisation provision to offset the loss of value and loss of income with regard to such securities. If the *Code des Assurances* considers this item as a liability to be covered by specific assets, the balance sheet will classify it as a *"réserve de capitalisation"* .

Technical provisions refer to:

1. premiums collected in advance;
2. benefits payable to the insured or to contract beneficiaries.

They may be classified in life as:

- **life insurance provisions** or **mathematical provisions**;
- provisions for unearned premiums, when separate from the following item;
- provisions for increasing risks, in long-term illness;
- provisions for bonuses,

and in non-life as:

- **provisions for unearned premiums**;
- **provisions for unexpired risks**, insofar as they are in addition to provisions for unearned premiums;
- **provisions for outstanding claims**.

In the United States, the term, "*provision*" is replaced by ***reserve***, which has two meanings:

1. technical provisions as in Europe, *e.g.* insurance reserves in **life insurance**, which equal the present value of future claims minus the present value of future **premiums** and premium and loss reserves in **non-life insurance**;

2. reserves in the conventional accounting sense, representing the portions of surplus appropriated to special accounts so that the corresponding assets will not be distributed as profits: *e.g.*, reserves for contingencies or for revaluation of assets.

TORT LAW SYSTEM

A ***tort*** is a civil wrong resulting in injury to a person or property. The standards and procedures by which torts are adjudicated constitute a country's **tort law system**. Torts can lead to three types of damages: economic (*e.g.*, lost wages or medical bills), non-economic (*e.g.*, awards for pain and suffering) and punitive (awards intended to punish the persons causing injury).

Torts are typically categorised as intentional, negligence or strict liability. An ***intentional tort*** is a legal wrong requiring actual or implied intent to do harm. Examples of intentional torts include assault, trespass on the property of another and nuisance (interference with the use and enjoyment of property). By contrast, the tort of ***negligence*** does not require intent to harm, but merely conduct that involves an unreasonable risk of causing injury to another person or damage to property. The required standard of care is what a reasonable person of ordinary prudence would do in the circumstances. For example, negligence occurs when an automobile is driven at an excessive speed and injures a passenger in another vehicle.

A third type of tort found in some jurisdictions is ***strict liability*** or liability without fault. The EU and the United States are the most prominent jurisdiction adopting strict liability torts. Strict liability is typically imposed in product liability cases and particularly hazardous activities. Under product liability theory, a person injured by a defective product can recover damages without having to prove that the manufacturer was negligent. The injured person needs only show that the product was defective when sold and that the defect caused injury. The tort defences of product abuse or misuse by the consumer, assumption of risk and comparative fault are typically available in product liability cases.

Civil and criminal liability for damage caused by defective products to individuals has been enacted in most EU member states following the ***Products Liability Directive***. The Product Liability Directive establishes a general duty of product safety and unambiguously requires the producer to establish safety as a high priority when designing, manufacturing and distributing products.

Most nations do not rely exclusively upon the tort system to help the injured. By blending indemnification aspects of insurance within the legal infrastructure, those injured by industrial or automobile accidents or by product defects are compensated without regard to the fault or culpability of the party causing the injury. In addition, national laws may impose fines and criminal liability on corporations with unsafe products and work places.

Most countries require motorists to carry liability insurance to compensate any injured party if the driver negligence causes injury. No-fault automobile statutes have been enacted in several countries. They are designed to soften some harsh effects of the tort system while reducing court congestion. The statutes provide generally that persons injured in automobile accidents are to be indemnified for their losses no matter who caused the accident. [see **COMPULSORY INSURANCE** and **POLICYHOLDER PROTECTION FUNDS (INSURANCE GUARANTY FUNDS)**]

As international interdependency grows, legal concepts based on differing cultural and economic and political systems will continue to evolve. Consider the mass tort class action, a United States procedural innovation that may be adopted in other countries. A ***class action*** is a procedure enacted to provide a means for a large group of injured persons to sue wrongdoers without identifying every group member in the lawsuit. The potential for massive damage awards is heightened through the use of this technique. As a result, many class action settlements are negotiated.

US courts have approved settlements of mass tort class action lawsuits involving asbestos-related diseases, breast implants and other product liability actions that restrict the rights of any future claimants to sue manufacturers or suppliers. The arrival of mass tort class actions has led the United States legal infrastructure to be besieged by political and institutional demands.

TRANSPARENCY

The fair-trade principle of **transparency** requires that regulatory and other legal requirements regarding **market access** and domestic operation should be clearly set out and easily available. Another dimension of transparency requires the ***tariffication*** of trade barriers; *i.e.*, the replacement of non-tariff trade barriers (*e.g.*, import quotas) with tariffs. Tariffication renders the cost of protectionism more transparent and can facilitate further negotiation to reduce protectionism. Many trade agreements further require signatory countries to ***bind the tariff*** (*i.e.*, to promise not to raise it).

Transparency problems exist in some insurance markets, with laws and **regulations** not clearly set out and readily available. Foreign firms can encounter transparency problems in countries which grant their insurance regulatory authorities broad discretionary powers, as the foreign insurer may have no clear understanding of the market access or operational requirements.

Many countries, especially those that have historically been relatively closed, may have unclear or non-existent due process. In which case, foreign (and domestic) insurers may not fully understand either their rights to appeal regulatory decisions or the process by which an appeal is launched.

UNDERWRITING CYCLE

The term **underwriting cycle** refers to the periodic swings in underwriting (technical) results observed in several **non-life insurance** markets. Such cycles are not found in the life branch and do not seem to exist in markets that are strictly regulated. Causes of cycles remain poorly understood. Traditional explanations focus on excess new capital flowing into the industry, catastrophic losses and stock market cycles. Recent research suggests institutional differences, **regulation**, interest rates and the general business cycle as factors.

Whatever the causes, cycles affect world-wide insurance and **reinsurance** capacity. Cycles have caused so-called capacity crises (or crunches). Such crises occur periodically within the non-life branch, such that some lines of insurance become scarce or even unavailable, a ***hard market***. With such market tightening, insurers can raise prices, and profits rise. Increased profit opportunities attract more capital into the business and induce managers to write more insurance with a given capital level. A ***soft market*** evolves, which is typically followed within five to eight years by another hard market. This oscillation can cause substantial disruption in some lines of insurance, giving rise to availability or affordability problems.

Although the existence of cycles in most markets is inconsistent with the rational expectations economic model, no evidence of industry-wide collusion exists.

Annex

OECD INSURANCE GUIDELINES FOR ECONOMIES IN TRANSITION

Introduction

The development of sound, modern and open insurance markets is a key component of financial reform in transition economies. Insurance plays a fundamental role in national economic and social structures as well as in the promotion of entrepreneurship spirit, which is so important for successful growth of emerging countries. Insurance companies are also major institutional investors, indispensable for the development and growth of capital markets. The financial importance of the insurance industry and its particular role in society evidently require the establishment of an adequate prudential and regulatory framework.

On the occasion of the Second East/West Conference on insurance systems in the economies in transition, held in Warsaw on 3-4 April 1997 under the aegis of the OECD's Centre for Co-operation with the Economies in Transition (CCET), seventeen economies in transition[1] and twenty-one OECD Member countries[2] held in-depth discussions on a broad range of policy issues of direct relevance for the development and modernisation of the insurance sector.

---

1. Albania, Armenia, Azerbaijan, Belarus, Bulgaria, Croatia, Estonia, Georgia, Latvia, Lithuania, Moldova, Mongolia, Uzbekistan, Romania, Slovak Republic, Slovenia, Ukraine.

2. Australia, Austria, Belgium, Finland, France, Germany, Hungary, Iceland, Japan, Korea, Luxembourg, Mexico, the Netherlands, Poland, Portugal, Spain, Sweden, Switzerland, Turkey, United Kingdom, United States.

A major outcome of this conference, which was organised by the OECD Insurance Committee with the Polish Government, was the endorsement by the thirty-eight participating countries of a set of twenty guidelines for insurance regulation and supervision in the economies in transition. This represents a major achievement for the CCET and for the OECD Insurance Committee, which has been at the forefront of promoting policy dialogue with, and providing technical assistance to, transition economies in the field of insurance.

Also, at the 58th session of the Insurance Committee held in November 1996, the OECD countries endorsed a more detailed document containing principles for insurance regulation and supervision in transition economies.

This annex contains both the twenty guidelines above-mentioned and the detailed principles. Its dissemination is intended to be of assistance to policy makers in emerging countries in their ongoing quest for modernising insurance regulatory and supervisory frameworks.

Twenty Insurance Guidelines

Rule n°1 Adequate prudential and regulatory provisions should be enforced in order to ensure the soundness of the insurance markets, the protection of the consumers and the stability of the economy as a whole. Over-regulation should be avoided. The insurance regulatory framework must be adapted to the characteristics of individual countries and encourage the stability, whilst maintaining the necessary flexibility to meet developments in the market.

Rule n°2 Sufficiently strict licensing criteria should govern the establishment of insurance companies. Among these criteria, the testing of the nature and adequacy of the financial resources of insurance companies, in particular through analysis of business plan and the requirement for a relevant minimum level of capital (taking account of inflation) deserves particular consideration. Other key requirements are related to the assessment of the ability of the company to meet legal, accounting and technical requirements and last but not least requirements for a competent management (fit and proper provisions).

Rule n°3 The underwriting of insurance risks should be restricted to insurance companies, which may transact insurance (and connected) operations only. Life and non-life activities should be separated (in distinct companies), so that one activity cannot be required to support the other. The distribution of insurance products by entities from other sectors may be authorised. Risks associated with the activities and structure of financial conglomerates should be adequately monitored.

Rule n°4 Establishment of foreign insurance companies should be based on prudential but non discriminatory rules. Liberalisation of cross-border operations, at least concerning reinsurance and international risks, should be encouraged.

Rule n°5 Adequate insurance contract laws should be established. Rules governing contractual rights and obligations as well as related sanctions, are essential for the protection of both contractual and third parties and indispensable for the development of legal stability. In the absence of contract laws, the approval of policy conditions by the supervisory authority may prove all the more necessary.

Rule n°6 Due to the crucial economic and social role of insurance in the development of an economy, consideration should be given to tax facilities in the life-insurance and pensions field in the economies in transition.

Rule n°7 The establishment of a supervisory body is essential. The supervisors should be professionally independent and properly trained and impartial. The supervisory body should have sufficient personnel and financial resources as well as adequate powers (including sanctions) to carry out its tasks.

Rule n°8 The examination of records and on site inspections of insurance companies are at the core of the work of the supervisor. An adequate reporting system is essential to achieve this task properly. The secrecy of information communication to and between supervisors should be safeguarded.

Rule n°9 Monitoring solvency margins and capital ratios constitutes a key element of dynamic supervision. But adequate tarification and prudent technical provisions backed by reliable and equivalent assets remain the fundamental requirements for maintaining solvency. Adequate business management and reinsurance activities are also indispensable to safeguard the soundness of the companies.

Rule n°10 Initially at least, it may be advisable for economies in transition to request the submission of premium rates and insurance products for prior approval. Supervision of tariffs and products should however be adapted to the particular situation of each country and reassessed at a later stage according to the development and progress of the market.

Rule n°11 Supervisory authorities should take adequate, effective and prompt measures to prevent insurance companies from defaulting, and to arrange an orderly run-off or the transfer of portfolio to a sound company. Appropriate winding-up procedures should be enforced. Under certain conditions, and particularly if the national market comprises a sufficient number of potential contributors with a broad spread of risks, the creation of a compensation fund could be considered.

Rule n°12 Standardised accounting rules are essential to ensure the transparency and comparability of the financial situation of insurance companies. Adequate insurance accounting rules and requirements for reporting and disclosure have to be set as a priority action. The compilation of statistical data regarding the frequency and severity of losses is an essential condition for computing tariffs and technical provisions accurately. Tariffs should be based on statistical data. Actuarial techniques are a key component of insurance management; the role of the actuarial profession could be encouraged.

Rule n°13 Investment regulation should ensure that both security and profitability requirements are respected. It should promote the diversification, spread and liquidity of investment portfolios as well as the maturity and currency matching of assets and liabilities, although some temporary dispensations to the last principle may be necessary. In any case, account should be taken of the country's current economic environment. Regulations might include a list of admitted assets on which ceilings may be set and requirements on the way in which investments should be valued.

Rule n°14 Regulation should not restrict free access to international reinsurance markets. Compulsory cessions of risks to domestic/national reinsurers should therefore be avoided. The collection and monitoring of information relating to reinsurance companies should be established. International co-operation is particularly important to obtain accurate information and should be strengthened.

Rule n°15 Insurance intermediaries should be registered in order to ensure their compliance with selected criteria. Insurance intermediaries should possess appropriate qualifications and provide adequate information to policyholders including disclosure of limits to their independence such as significant ties with insurance companies. Insurance brokers should possess either financial guarantees or professional liability insurance.

Rule n°16 Compulsory insurance may be justified in respect of certain forms of social protection and might be considered in other areas where the risks covered are particularly serious, or where premium payments should be divided on an equitable basis among the policyholders group under consideration. Compulsory insurance is particularly recommended for automobile third party liability. Guarantee funds could be created to compensate victims when there is no insurance cover. Tariffs for compulsory insurance should also be based on statistical data. Adequate monitoring systems should be established. Compulsory insurance should not be restricted to former monopolies or State owned companies.

Rule n°17 Regulations should allow for fair competition within the insurance and reinsurance market. The process of dismantling monopolies and the privatisation of government owned insurance companies should be strongly encouraged.

Rule n°18 The activities of insurance companies in the pensions and health insurance field should be encouraged within an appropriate regulatory and supervisory framework. Regulations should endeavour to ensure fair treatment between all private companies operating in these areas.

Rule n°19 Governments should strengthen co-operation in order to exchange information on insurance regulation and supervision, facilitate the monitoring of the activities of foreign insurance and reinsurance companies and promote the development of sound, modern and open insurance markets.

Rule n°20 The insurance industry should be encouraged to set up its own business guidelines and to develop adequate training structures. Self-regulatory principles and organisations, including professional bodies, can complement usefully the public supervisory structure.

Principles of Insurance Regulation and Supervision in Economies in Transition

Although general guiding principles can be set forth for the benefit of the regulatory and supervisory authorities of countries in transition, those principles are applicable only if they are adapted to the economic environment as well as to the historical and cultural context of each country. Specifically, a number of regulations enforced in countries where the insurance sector has attained an advanced degree of maturity can only be progressively incorporated into economies in transition. Also, certain regulatory provisions that have long existed in OECD countries, but are nowadays no longer justified due to changes in the economic and regulatory environment of those countries, may be appropriate in light of the current stage of development of certain countries in transition.

In addition, insurance regulations should be flexible so as to evolve in accordance with changes in the economic environment and the insurance market. For that reason, it could be appropriate to incorporate certain provisions not in the law itself but rather in implementing regulations that are easier to amend. Maintaining this margin of flexibility is also perfectly compatible with preserving legal predictability, which economic agents require.

In order for the regulations to have the desired effect, they should stipulate obligations as well as provide for realistic penalties in the event of non-compliance with thc applicable statutory and regulatory provisions.

Finally, special mention should be made of the importance of having different regulations applying to life and non-life insurance. Each of those branches operates under its own constraints and requires specific management and regulatory structures.

The paragraphs which follow contain observations concerning some of the fundamental aspects of insurance regulation and supervision to be addressed by economies in transition. The order and length of these paragraphs should not be taken as an indication of their relative importance as regards the policies governing insurance.

Licensing

Sufficiently strict conditions governing the formal approval of insurance companies serve to guarantee the protection of insurance users and ensure that fair, competitive conditions exist among companies in the domestic market. In most OECD countries, separate licenses are issued for each class of insurance (or for several classes grouped under a common denomination) usually in the six months following the filing of applications, and they are generally permanent.

Experts agree on the importance of a certain number of criteria that must be met by an insurer seeking to be licensed. Among those, the first may be the strict testing of the nature and adequacy of the financial resources of insurance companies at the time they go into business, an essential condition for ensuring that they have the financial strength needed to operate. The minimum required capital is that which would enable a company to meet certain contingencies inherent in its business. The amount of such capital (expressed in a manner that takes inflation into account) varies according to the insurance class in question and to the specific conditions prevailing in different markets. Lastly, a deposit, either of a fixed or variable amount, may be required in addition to the minimum capital requirement.

In addition to these financial standards, economies in transition should not fail to impose other licensing criteria, which have been used in all OECD countries. They concern in particular:

- legal requirements, i.e., in particular, conformity of the form of business organisation adopted by the company, filing of bylaws and general terms and conditions of policies, insurance specialisation;
- accounting requirements, i.e. filing of opening balance sheet, budget and income statement, proof that the company has the required minimum capital, etc.;
- technical requirements, i.e. filing of premium rates for information or, if applicable, for approval, as well as of the technical bases used in tarification and planned technical provisions, and of reinsurance contracts;
- managerial requirements, i.e. demonstration that officers are fit and proper, and that the shareholders are reputable.

Supervision of insurance companies

In many economies in transition policyholders are highly vulnerable because they lack access to reliable information on products, intermediaries and insurance companies, while insurers are still short on training and experience and there can be significant gaps in regulatory coverage. The implementation of adequate supervision for the insurance sector would be a first step towards removing those deficiencies.

Regardless of which structure is chosen for supervisory bodies (independent authority, ministry of finance division, etc.), experts in charge of supervising insurance companies must be properly trained and impartial.

The examination of records is at the core of the work of supervisors. They analyse records supplied by insurance firms and may request any additional accounting or business document they deem necessary for their audit. Thorough on-site investigations are an indispensable complement of audits of records. *A priori* supervision is also particularly recommended in countries where economic structures and comprehensive regulations have not yet been developed. The prevention and detection of insurers' financial problems would enable the supervisory authorities of countries in transition not only to safeguard the solvency of companies, but also, in a more general way, to promote public confidence in recently privatised institutions within a business sector about which the public may still be unfamiliar.

The duties of supervisory authorities should focus on the following general areas:

- supervision with respect to legal obligations: compliance with existing legal provisions, by-laws of the company, general terms and conditions of insurance policies;
- financial supervisions: own funds, technical provisions, assets, monitoring of business activities;
- audit of interim and annual financial statements;
- actuarial supervision: tariffs, technical or mathematical provisions;
- management supervision: fit and proper requirements of company officers, reputation of strategic shareholders;
- economic supervision: conditions prevailing in the marketplace, statistics.

Initially at least, it may be advisable in economies in transition to submit premium rates for prior approval. This practice would efficiently safeguard the financial soundness of insurance companies, which might otherwise be tempted to engage in rate wars, thereby running the risk of putting their solvency in jeopardy. On the other hand, excessively high tariffs would penalise policyholders. Above all, in economies in transition, the lack of experience of insurance management, combined with the shortage of basic statistical data such as the frequency and severity of losses, can make it difficult or, indeed, impossible to set premiums rates based on actual risk exposure.

Regulatory and supervisory authorities may therefore have to draft regulations on premium rates on the basis of probability assumptions. In addition, they will have to compensate for the difficulty of individual data collection by seeing to it that a national body of statistics is being established.

Similarly, it seems advisable that the insurance products offered for sale be examined by the supervisory authority, so that consumers will not be harmed by inappropriate policy conditions. The risk of asymmetry in the information available to the insurer and to the insured is even greater in economies in transition, due to insufficient disclosure of information on insurance products and companies.

Supervision of premium rates and policy conditions must however be adapted to the particular situation of each country, and reassessed at a later stage according to the development and progress of the market.

Prudential rules in OECD countries also include requirements for solvency thresholds or margins which correspond to the minimum amount of capitalisation required for the type of business written by the company, in order to cope with the contingencies associated with that business or to offset any shortfalls in the technical provisions set aside. That margin, which is computed for individual companies on the basis of their commitments, constitutes the first step towards dynamic supervision. It may be appropriate for it to reflect as much as possible the nature and diversity of the risks to which the company is exposed, using as models those recently developed by certain OECD Member countries. Nevertheless, a solvency margin that matches regulatory standards should not be deemed by the management or supervisory authority to be the end-result of the assets-liabilities management and a fail-safe guarantee of the financial soundness of the company under consideration. Furthermore, the mechanism for setting margins may be affected in a situation of high inflation.

Above all, the margin is only an instrument for measuring and monitoring solvency; adequate tarification, investments that correspond to technical commitments and sufficient technical provisions remain the main pillars of solvency.

The setting aside of technical (or mathematical) provisions in an amount sufficient to meet at all times the company's commitments vis-à-vis the insured remains at the very core of insurance business. Most countries have agreed on the definition of technical provisions to be set aside. Among those, the following non-life provisions can be quoted: provisions for unearned premiums, provisions for unexpired risks, provisions for claims outstanding or equalisation reserves.

The method used for setting the amount of these provisions, whether imposed or regulated, should be based on national statistical data. At first, it is likely that computing for the purpose of setting technical provisions will have to be based on probability assumptions, owing to the absence of reliable nation-wide statistics (such as mortality tables for life insurance) in most countries in transition.

It seems essential that the supervisory authorities be given adequate sanction powers in the event insurers fail to comply with legal provisions governing the setting aside of technical provisions. Under these circumstances, it would in particular be advisable that a company no longer has the unrestricted use of its assets.

More generally, in order to perform adequately its duties, the supervisory authority will have to develop an on-going dialogue with insurers so as to appear as a partner of companies' success, instead of being confined to a coercive role.

Investments

In OECD countries, regulations governing the management of assets are based on a list of "admissible" investments. In order to ensure that requirements of both safety and profitability are respected, countries in transition may also adopt a series of principles (listed below), which have proved useful in this respect in more advanced markets.

Diversification, spread and liquidity

Ceilings may be set on admitted investments, by type of investment and in percentage terms rather than in absolute value, so as to reduce the risk of default or of liquidity shortages associated with certain types of investments, as well as to ensure that portfolios are sufficiently diversified. A ceiling may also be set for given investments (according to the principle of spreading investments within each category). Although OECD countries now very seldom set floor limits, such practices were sometimes used in the past, especially to encourage investments with a low risk of loss or lack of liquidity.

When setting ceilings, the impact of the method used for establishing the value of investments must be taken into consideration (for example through a prudent assessment of investments). Lastly, insurance companies are generally advised against having recourse to debt to finance long-term investments.

At this stage, regulatory and supervisory authorities should make sure that a distinction applies between the treatment of investments representing technical reserves and that of investments of the capital base. The latter has a role to play in the long run, particularly with respect to the funding of the company's future growth, and it would be sound policy to let companies earn a high return on the investment of their capital base, so that they may reinforce their financial resources. However, the buffer effect of the capital base in its role as a complement to technical provisions and possible equalisation reserves may serve as grounds for justifying restrictions placed on investments of these funds. Thus, one will also have to distinguish, within owners' equity itself, between the minimum required capital and the free capital. While there is a need for regulations on the investment of the minimum capital - which ought to be readily available to pay exceptionally high claims - those concerning the investment of the free capital seem less justified.

Localisation

The domestic location and/or custody of certificates of investments corresponding to technical reserves can be of particular importance in countries in transition. This makes it possible for them to ward off two problems to which they may be exposed more frequently than OECD countries, namely difficulties in establishing proof of ownership and the possibility of fraud by companies. Those provisions should not constitute an obstacle to the balance of investments.

Currency matching

The currency matching rule refers to the fact that investments ought to be in the same currency as commitments. In the case of economies in transition, the current fragility of their national currency as compared to those of foreign countries in which foreign investments can be made, may lead to tolerate a certain degree of flexibility. Regulations should simply state in what foreign currencies investments may be made. Also, arguments in favour of the matching of currencies in which the shareholders' equity of companies is invested are less convincing. Lastly, the fact that a national currency is fragile justifies even more that insurers and reinsurers should at least be authorised to hold foreign-currency reserves in the amount of their commitments payable in those currencies; this is the case, for instance, for reinsurance policies between domestic insurers and foreign reinsurance companies.

Maturity matching

One of the primary objectives of insurance companies in managing their assets, in particular in the life-insurance sector, is to ensure that the maturity of those assets matches that of their commitments, so as to reduce the risk of changes in interest rates. Partial and temporary exemptions from that rule may be considered in certain countries, given their economic situation (tightness of capital markets, rampant inflation, concerns about investments in domestic securities, etc.).

Insolvency and management of troubled companies

Clear instructions should exist regarding what is to be done about insolvent insurers through legislation covering all matters connected with the management of troubled companies, including standards used to establish insolvency, the basis for choosing between rehabilitation and liquidation, recovery measures available (premium rate increase, freezing of assets, request for reinsurance plans, injection of capital, etc.), the revocation of licenses, conditions under which policies may be transferred to a sound company (often resulting in the rights of policyholders being safeguarded), the role of the liquidator and the ranking of creditors' claims.

In most OECD countries, it is generally accepted that supervisory authorities should do everything in their power to prevent an insurance company from defaulting, as this would be damaging to the entire insurance sector.

Some countries have also opted in favour of guarantee funds which pay the claims of insolvent companies. However, in countries in transition, the advisability of creating such a fund should be assessed by looking at its costs, which could weaken participating companies, and at the possible aggravation of moral hazard that the establishment of such a fund may cause - as compared with the possible benefits derived from it.

Liberalisation and competition in the insurance sector

While implementing a programme of removing monopolies and privatising state-owned companies, economies in transition are preparing for the advent of a globally competitive insurance market. In this connection, the regulatory and supervisory authorities of countries in transition would be well advised to ensure that state-owned companies and private firms are treated equally, although it may be justifiable to hold on to certain exclusive rights, such as in the field of export credits and political risks, which are generally areas covered by companies run by the state.

The danger inherent in a policy of closed markets should also be underscored, and competition encouraged, free of discrimination based on companies' nationality. The presence of subsidiaries or branches of foreign insurers, as well as the acquisition by foreign companies of minority or majority interests (the restriction of ownership to a minority of the shares may dissuade foreign companies from entering the market), contribute to the development of the domestic insurance sector. Foreign presence brings with it innovation and transfers of know-how, while at the same time giving access to additional financial resources, improving insurance rules, fostering greater diversification of business, expanding capacity so that a steep growth in demand will not be held back by the small size of the domestic insurance sector, broadening the scope of products offered and increasing financial security, to mention only the main advantages. While prudential regulation of investment is necessary, discriminatory provisions or practices which would constitute obstacles to investments by foreign insurance companies should be avoided and the adoption is recommended of a relatively liberal attitude towards exchange controls.

Distribution of insurance products

The emergence of new insurance companies and new insurance products requires the development of modern distribution networks, with the possibility of an adequate combination of several types of intermediaries (insurance company staff, agents, brokers, direct sales, etc.). Considering that in many cases only intermediaries have contact with consumers, it might be recommended that regulations covering intermediaries be adopted, at least insofar as brokers are concerned (insurance companies being often in a position to exercise at least indirect control over agents). These regulations would cover issues such as registration, required business qualifications and ethical standards, along with financial security (including the need for professional liability coverage).

Supervisory authorities should see to it that intermediaries conduct their business as transparently as possible; specifically, they should disclose to their clients their status on any ties that they may have to insurance companies, along with providing extensive information on, and explanations of, policies to policyholders.

Insurance accounting

Accurate accounting provides authorities with the practical means to perform proper supervision, while at the same time being a resourceful instrument for the management of companies.

Widely available financial statements and proper financial information are important assets both for the supervisory authorities and the insurance market. That is why, in OECD countries, insurers are required by law to issue financial statements certified by an independent auditor as fair and accurate.

There is no doubt as to the advantage of standardising accounting rules at the national level in terms of disclosure and comparability of the financial positions of companies (this concerns mainly the presentation of annual financial statements, evaluation rules, the contents of notes to the financial statements and of the annual report, the presentation of consolidated financial statements, auditing and publication, as well as sanction measures).

Among the accounting problems encountered in economies in transition, those having to do with valuation and assessments are particularly thorny. The evaluation of technical commitments should for instance be made through several approaches involving looking at past and future performance. In several countries in transition, owing to the absence of a genuine market, prudential rules may play a particularly important role in the valuation of assets, regardless of the assessment method used (none has been universally endorsed, even within the OECD, where certain countries use book/acquisition value and others emphasise market value). In addition, a periodic reassessment of certain assets, such as buildings, seems necessary. Lastly, it is important to make allowance for inflation, which is high in many of those economies and makes it even more difficult to keep a prudent and fair accounting that accurately reflects the financial position of companies.

Statistics

The compiling of nation-wide statistical data, particularly regarding the frequency and severity of losses (mortality tables in life insurance) is a *sine qua non* condition for computing tariffs and technical reserves accurately. Compiling could be done by the supervisory authority or by a specialised body. It would make sense that it focuses initially on key insurance classes, such as automobile liability insurance and fire insurance.

Furthermore, the creation of a reliable statistical instrument is the only way for insurance companies to demonstrate to the tax authorities that they are justified in setting aside certain amounts to cover their commitments.

Contract law

In an environment where markets are opening up, the insurance sector is rapidly expanding, and the number of participants and complexity of products are on the rise, the protection of insurance policyholders in economies in transition also requires the enactment of a contract law or the improvement of the existing one. It is a way for lawmakers to bring the rights and obligations of the parties into balance and to devise sanction measures proportionate to the violations committed.

A certain number of general principles, which served as guidelines for the enactment of contract laws in OECD countries, may be listed for the benefit of countries in transition. For instance, the distinction between policies providing for indemnities and those paying flat sums should be clear, including the various legal consequences thereof (differences in the amount of compensation in the event of a loss in particular). The importance of establishing the exact time at which contracts are executed and go into effect, their life, as well as the issue of proof of contract, should also be underscored. A contract implies obligations on the part of the company but also on that of the insured, including that of declaring loss exposure (and the possible aggravation thereof), paying premiums and reporting damages or losses. The possibility that a policyholder may be underinsured should not be overlooked, anymore than that of intentional losses or wrongful conduct, which constitute grounds for exclusion from coverage. In order to be complete, insurance contract law also needs to refer to the rights of third parties to compensation or with respect to the insurer, as well as providing for the modalities of disputes settlement.

Besides the technical aspects of contract law, some leeway is left for each government to determine the degree of protection it wishes to provide for policyholders, with due regard to the cost of restrictions under consideration and to the supervisory capabilities they require.

Compulsory insurance

Insurance is made compulsory out of a desire to protect the whole or part of the public. In addition, compulsory insurance enables the state to cease being financially responsible for certain losses which they otherwise would have to compensate.

With the exception of automobile liability, it is hard to suggest for which kind of risks insurance cover should be compulsory. The need for certain types of compulsory insurance will be appraised differently from one country to another. At most, it can be stated that compulsory insurance seems advisable in the case of the following types of cover:

- in branches which are more closely related to the social sector than to private insurance;
- in specific areas where compulsory insurance is justified by the seriousness of risk exposure and/or by its generalised nature (automobile liability or occupational accidents for instance);
- in areas where premium payments should be divided on an equitable basis among the policyholders group under consideration.

Lastly, insurance can reasonably be made compulsory only in those sectors for which effective oversight is available at a reasonable cost.

Concern for losses incurred by third parties may also justify the implementation of mechanisms that serve to compensate for non-compliance with insurance requirements, or for the default of an insurer (e.g. guarantee fund for automobile liability insurance).

In most instances, the setting of uniform rates is not required, since competition will normally have an impact in the field of compulsory insurance as for other insurance categories. Should it be deemed preferable to set rates, it is important that tariffs take into account available statistical data and the economic situation of the sector under consideration.

Specialisation

Specialisation by companies along the lines of life and non-life insurance ensures that assets are managed separately and that losses incurred, for instance, in the non life-insurance sector will not affect life policyholders.

At the inter-sectoral level, the experience of OECD countries calls for prudence with respect to structures of the bank/insurance type, at least at this stage of development of the markets of economies in transition. The technical specificities of these businesses (such as that of non-life insurance for instance, whose management is highly complex, both in the setting of insurance premium levels and in assessing claims and how to compensate for them), along with the specificity of prudential rules applicable to the insurance sector, the risk of transfers of credit or dividends, exposure to conflicts of interest, contagion involving various constituent parts of a conglomerate or double gearing are just some of the reasons why these structures should be carefully monitored.

Taxation of life insurance

In light of the potential economic and social role of life insurance in countries in transition as well as of the obstacles to the purchase of life insurance (high rate of inflation, absence of insurance culture, very high nominal interest paid on cash savings, lack of knowledge about products, impossibility to guarantee an attractive rate of return on long-term policies, etc.) the establishment of tax incentives may be considered in order to promote this market. Incentives could for instance come in the form of tax deductions or credits for premiums paid by individuals on certain policies. Premiums paid by employers on policies providing reasonable life-insurance benefits on behalf of employees could also be tax deductible by employers and employees would not have to pay taxes on them.

Lastly, regardless of the tax model selected, it seems particularly advisable to keep its administration very simple in countries which often lack the means to enforce tax compliance.

Actuaries

The complexity and specific nature of actuarial work warrants encouraging the promotion of the actuarial profession. Actuaries can contribute in a useful way to the performance of very important tasks by insurance companies, such as calculating premium rates, calculating the amount of technical provisions, assessing contractual obligations, as well as preparing financial reports, monitoring solvency margins, developing insurance products, consulting on investment strategies, participating in the development of computer systems or making arrangements for reinsurance. In almost all OECD countries, insurance companies are required by law to appoint actuaries. This precaution seems all the more relevant at an initial stage, in order for this profession to be recognised.

Reinsurance

Adequate and effective reinsurance enables insurance companies to share risks with others, limit losses from large risks and, in a more general way, to streamline their risk portfolio and to allocate technical income and expenses over time. In many ways, such objectives are incompatible with regulations still in effect in certain economies in transition, in particular those concerning the compulsory cession of reinsurance. Only through free access to the wider international reinsurance market can the ceding company be ensured of getting the best product at a competitive price.

In addition, supervisory authorities should endeavour to protect insurers against the collapse of reinsurers. Supervisory authorities could start out by monitoring reinsurance transactions through an audit of the financial statements and notes thereto (in particular reinsurance agreements) of ceding companies. It is also very useful to compile as much information as possible on reinsurers, their solvency and liquidity (including through rating agencies), as well as, more generally, on the overall impact of ceding risks, taking into consideration all significant transactions with respect to claims, commissions and brokers' fees. Supervisory authorities from different countries may wish to consider working closely together in this area.

Private pension systems

The governments of OECD countries as well as of many economies in transition are experiencing growing difficulties in supporting pay-as-you-go pension systems. Current pension systems are therefore bound to be revised, while funded systems should grow in importance. In this context, the private sector will become responsible for a progressively larger share of pensions. At a macro-economic level, this trend is expected to provide a powerful boost to long-term savings. Hence, consideration could be given, among others, to tax incentives and regulations aimed at promoting the establishment of employee pension plans by employers. The role played by insurance companies in the financing of private pension systems will also have to be examined.

BIBLIOGRAPHY

OECD (1999), *Liberalisation of International Insurance Operations: Cross-border Trade and Establishment of Foreign Branches*

OECD (1999), *Insurance Regulation and Supervision in OECD Countries.*

OECD (1999), *Insurance Statistics Yearbook, 1990-1997*

OECD (1999), *Insurance regulation and supervision in Asian countries*

OECD (1997), *Insurance Regulation and Supervision in Economies in Transition*

OECD (1997), *Code of Liberalisation of Current Invisible Operations*

OECD (1997), *Code of Liberalisation of Capital Movements*

OECD (1996), *Policy Issues in Insurance: Investment, Taxation, Insolvency*

OECD (1995), *Insurance Solvency Supervision*

OECD (1993), *Policy Issues in Insurance*

OECD (1992), *Insurance and other financial services: structural trends*

INDEX

D

E

F

G

H

I

L

M

N

O

P

Q

R

S

T

U

V

W

X

OECD PUBLICATIONS, 2, rue André-Pascal, 75775 PARIS CEDEX 16
PRINTED IN FRANCE
(14 1999 02 1 P) ISBN 92-64-17083-9 – No. 50711 1999